all my "Berry

Shari

psalm 84:11

BERRIED IN

Chocolate

BERRIED IN
Chocolate

How I Built a Multimillion-Dollar Business by Doing What I Love to Do and How You Can Too

by
Shari Fitzpatrick

Foreword by
Jennifer Openshaw

PELICAN PUBLISHING COMPANY
Gretna 2011

*The word "Pelican" and the depiction of a pelican are
trademarks of Pelican Publishing Company, Inc., and are
registered in the U.S. Patent and Trademark Office.*

Library of Congress Cataloging-in-Publication Data

Fitzpatrick, Shari.
   Berried in chocolate : how I built a multimillion-dollar business by
doing what I love to do and how you can too / by Shari Fitzpatrick.
       p. cm.
    ISBN 978-1-58980-881-2 (hardcover : alk. paper) 1. Fitz-
patrick, Shari. 2. Businesswomen—United States—Biography. 3.
Women-owned business enterprises—United States. 4. New business enterprises—United States. I. Title.

   HC102.5.F54A3 2011
   338.7'6648047—dc22
   [B]

                                                    2010043643

*The New Living Translation of the Bible has been used for references
throughout this book.*

Printed in the United States of America
Published by Pelican Publishing Company, Inc.
1000 Burmaster Street, Gretna, Louisiana 70053

This book is dedicated to my sister-in-law, Emily, who taught me how to dip strawberries in chocolate; my mom, Joan (who not only named me but also my business), whose support, prayers, and love have been priceless; and of course my amazing husband and the love of my life, Clay, and our three wonderful boys, Paxton, Hogan, and Max. Thank you for giving me clear proof that God answers prayers.

Contents

Foreword

I know what it's like to be juggling it all: mom, maker of meals, mobile machine, and moneymaker. Now more than ever, women are the doers; it's why we often need encouragement and inspiration. As I've seen too many times, women can do anything we put our minds to, but sometimes we need that shining light to keep us moving forward.

I first learned about Shari Fitzpatrick when I lived in Sacramento, California. When I was writing *The Millionaire Zone,* I knew that her story of turning her own passion into profits was a perfect fit for real, everyday Americans. Shari's down-to-earth, can-do attitude has resonated with and encouraged countless entrepreneurs across the country. Shari isn't someone who came from "something"; she isn't even someone who came from a big city. She is someone who came from within herself, within her own passion. That's something that each and every one of us—every one of you—has. But women who are juggling work and families know that it's never easy. No, success doesn't come easily. In this book, though, Shari takes you through her ups and downs, the good and the bad, the mistakes and the successes. She gives you real examples of what building a business is about—not just what you read in magazines, but what it's really like on the inside.

Shari is truly a "Zoner." She has learned the importance of a "Lifenet" (no one does it alone), recognizing that success can come from failure and that giving back is an essential component in the march toward reaching our full potential. Isn't that what life is about—reaching our potential?

Shari's inspirational story gives insight and direction to anyone considering building a business by starting from their passion!

Jennifer Openshaw
CEO of SuperFutures, columnist for Dow Jones' MarketWatch,
and author of *The Millionaire Zone*

Acknowledgments

As I wrote in this book, no one does it alone. I am so grateful for the support of my family, friends, and business associates, many of whom you'll read about in these pages. But there are so many more! Here are just some of them:

General Produce, my strawberry supplier since the beginning, who has taken such great care of me—special thanks to *Gerald, Mike, Cliff,* and *Tom . . . Terry Wong,* the genius "wind beneath my wings" on my new product venture, who showed his confidence in me . . . the three winemakers who have supported my wine efforts, *Michael Beem, John Miller,* and the owner of *Perry Creek Winery, Dieter Juergens . . . Mike and "D" Iverson,* owners of Iverson Winery . . . *Brian and Diana Fitzpatrick,* owners of Fitzpatrick Winery . . .

The best florist in Sacramento, *Kim Hoskinson at Blossoms & Balloons,* who was my mentor during my early business years and who became a great friend whom I can always rely on for advice on my creative ideas . . . *Lynda Strong,* my amazing vendor, who helps us find many of our packaging solutions . . . *Dave Chambers,* the manager of wonderful Sacramento restaurants, who is always willing to take care of my staff during the holidays or me and my family just dropping in . . . *Steve and Julie Ryan,* the owners of *Rudy's Hideaway Restaurant* in Sacramento—we enjoy each other's products and have become good friends over the years . . . *Greg and Mary Kemp,* owners and operators of my neighborhood restaurant *The Gold Vine Grill,* who helped me with the recipe projects for this book—Greg is one of the greatest chefs in the world . . .

Steve Dominguez, my banker and friend . . . *Dick Pennell,* my investment banker and friend . . . *Mary Burroughs,* my graphic designer

11

and friend . . . *John Fitzpatrick* and *Tonya Casimiro*, my accountants . . . my incredible lawyers, *Michael Kvarme* and *Scott Hervey*, the "berry best" attorneys in Sacramento, who protected and represented me against "Goliath" . . . *Don Bonner of Western Design Tile Company*, my friend and supporter . . . *Hal Hammond*, my very first graphics guy, who helped me so much in the beginning . . . *Zaida Klein*, a Shari's Berries International (SBI) board member who became a wonderful friend and who supported me through the SBI nightmare, counseling me numerous times through some very tough situations—her support and friendship have been priceless and God-sent . . . *Dr. Anne Marie Adams*, my doctor, who has taken such great care of me and is my close Christian friend . . . *Ted Nugent*, who supports me by being a fool for my berries, even acknowledging me in *his* book—I just know my new line of frozen cherries will become his new favorite . . .

Lynda Clayton, one of Sacramento's great radio personalities, who has been a supporter of me and my company since the beginning, giving me marketing opportunities and praying for my success—we are often mistaken for sisters, which we are in the Lord . . . all my friends at *Sacramento Magazine*, including *Bret Conners*, my friend and sales rep, and *Joe Chiodo*, co-publisher . . . all Sacramento area radio, TV, and newspaper people who have helped me over the years, including but not limited to *Jeff Holden, Kitty O'Neal, Ed Crane, Grant Napear, Bob Shallit, Darrell Smith, Blair Anthony Robertson, Jennifer Smith, Marianne McClary, Tina Macuha, Nick Tomé, Paul Robins, Lizann Hunt, Kelly Johnson, Jeff Tarbell, John Nelson, Amy Bingham, Matt Vierra, Mark S. Allen, Darla Givens, Lee Perkins, and Andrea Gomez* . . .

Dahlynn McKowen, writer and author who chose me to be featured in *Chicken Soup for the Entrepreneur's Soul*, which led me to be on Sandra Yancey's show . . . *Sandra Yancey*, who asked me to speak at the annual eWomenNetwork Conference, where I had the chance to meet and be inspired by Jan King . . . *Jan King*, founder and editorial director of *eWomenPublishingNetwork*—without Jan I could never have pulled off this book deal . . . *Laurel Marshfield* of *Blue Horizon Communications*, who put my great book proposal together . . . *Kim Pearson* of *Primary Sources*, the outstanding writer who helped me write this book . . . *Pelican Publishing Company*, who offered me a publishing deal not only because they knew a good thing when they saw it—I knew they were the right publisher for me because not only are they great publishers but the mascot of Klamath Falls High School, where I was a cheerleader, was the pelican . . .

My bookkeeper, *Sheri Farley,* who has worked with me since the 1990s . . . and Sheri's daughter *Nicki Farley Kitchen,* also known as "Nit" by my boys when she was their nanny, who loves my boys almost as much as I do—today she is married and is a great home-maker with several children of her own . . . my close friend and father figure, *George Moore,* who never got to read this book because he passed away before I shared it with him in its grand final form—but I know he is reading it in heaven . . . all of my amazing employees who have stayed with me through the good times and the difficult times, especially my right-hand girl and voice of reason *Glenda,* plus *Don, Deb, Jessica,* and *ReNida* . . . all my friends and family who have prayed for me and my family and helped me over the years—many of them donate their time during the holidays just to "help me" . . . my amazing friend and Bible study teacher, *Debbie Kientz,* who gener-ously shared her in-depth knowledge of the Bible to help me edit all my faith references . . .

Finally, I am especially grateful to my *Lord Jesus Christ.* Without His direction over my life, I could not be who I am today, blessed throughout the years in good times and in bad.

Introduction

The Right Time

Some people call me the "Strawberry Lady," which is fine with me. But that's not who I've always been. Once upon a time I was a stockbroker, back in the late 1980s when young female stockbrokers were pretty rare.

I liked my prestigious job title, and I wasn't the only one. My then-boyfriend Clay got a charge out of referring to "my girlfriend, you know, the stockbroker." Nobody else he knew had a stockbroker for a girlfriend. He was proud of me—and I was proud that he was proud.

So it probably came as a not-so-pleasant shock to him when I announced one night that I wanted to quit my great job as a stockbroker and instead dip strawberries in chocolate for a living.

I wanted to start my own berry-dipping company and make it my *career*—seriously.

We were cuddling on the couch when I dropped this happy bombshell. Since my head was on his shoulder, I couldn't see his face, but it got really, really quiet. It stayed quiet for a couple of minutes.

Finally, he gently patted my shoulder and said carefully, "Honey, maybe now is not the right time." Clay has always been supportive of whatever I wanted to do, but I could tell he was finding it a little difficult to be supportive of someone who might have just lost her mind.

But to his everlasting credit, he didn't say no or that it was a bad idea. He didn't laugh in my face or throw a bunch of economic facts at me proving how dumb this would be. I'm not saying he didn't think these things, but he didn't say them. He still reminds me of this fact today.

In 2002, I received an award as Sacramento's Businesswoman of the Year, in front of 1,500 people at a fancy sit-down dinner at the

Hyatt Regency Hotel. Clay, by then my husband and the father of our three sons, was in the audience as I walked to the podium to receive the award as the founder of Shari's Berries, the leading brand of dipped strawberries in the nation.

I just couldn't resist closing my acceptance remarks by saying, "Honey, it *was* the right time."

I have trouble believing it has been that long since I started my chocolate-dipped strawberry business. Those years seemed to scoot by me while I was too busy to notice. In 1989, when the business began, I was so young—twenty-five—that I didn't know it was impossible to do what I did. My financing consisted of a $1,500 cash advance on a credit card. I dipped strawberries by myself out of my tiny kitchen in a one-bedroom apartment, and I delivered them myself. In 2008, the two brands I created were sold from retail stores and Web sites, with over 2.5 million hand-dipped strawberries filling about 250,000 gift boxes from multiple warehouses. Since my first company began, over 14 million gourmet dipped strawberries have been shipped all over the country. I am recognized as a leader in the gourmet-food gift industry.

Most customers who meet me are shocked at my appearance. They say, "You're so young!" They expect me to be a little old gray-haired lady, like Mrs. See of See's Candies. I suppose I am a little younger than most who write their memoirs, but for me this is another "right time." Life has given me a lot. It's the right time for me to give some back. A book seems like a good way to share what I've learned along the way. And I want to tell you my story because if I can be successful, so can you.

It's a little scary to write a book about your life. This time it's not just my strawberries "out there"—it's me! But my friends and family will tell you that I'm a risk-taker kind of gal. I'll get on any kind of roller coaster no matter how scary, high, or fast. Usually I'll drag someone along with me and scare them half to death while I enjoy every minute of the thrill. It's fun out here on the edge!

Here's a secret: life *is* fun. This is the number-one thing I want to share. Laugh more often. Let other people wow your socks off—and tell them when they do. Give lots of presents. Eat more strawberries, especially when they've been dipped and decorated.

This book isn't arranged in chronological order, as in "this happened first and then that and then that." Life lessons don't come in such neat and tidy packages. Sometimes we have to take many "classes" in many different "schools" before we learn something. So the book is arranged around a dozen important lessons that life has taught me. It mixes up my personal life and my business life—I'm a wife, mom, daughter, sister, and friend as well as an entrepreneur, business owner, marketing guru, and even amateur entertainer (or as some might say, a natural-born ham).

But I don't want you to get lost among my jumbled memories, so just to make sure you know where you are, here's a brief timeline to help you follow my story.

It began in Klamath Falls, a small town in southern Oregon, where I was born in 1964 and where nearly all of my family still lives today. My parents were divorced when I was seven, and my mother married my stepfather, Ben, about a year later. My sister, Dayna, and I joined Ben's three sons, Rick, Mike, and Bruce, making a Brady Bunch blended family. I graduated from the same high school my father and grandmother attended, not to mention my uncles, sister, brothers, and now nephews. I met the love of my life in high school, and although we broke up for a time, we got married right before my ten-year high school reunion. Our moms still live a mile away from each other in Klamath Falls.

I have no formal business education. I left home to attend college in Eugene, Oregon, not so much to get an education as to get over being dumped by my boyfriend. (Yes, it was Clay, the same supportive guy I ended up marrying ten years later.) College wasn't really for me, so in 1985 at the age of twenty I left to become rich and famous in glamorous California. I had no idea how I was going to do this, only that I knew it was sure to happen somehow.

In my search for what I was going to be when I grew up, I tried a lot of things—would-be stewardess, waitress, sales clerk, mortgage broker, time-shares saleswoman, photographer, and stockbroker. I moved from Los Angeles to Reno to Sacramento. I was successful, meaning I proved I could make money, but the fun wasn't there. The most fun I had was from my hobby of making fancy gift baskets filled with chocolate-dipped strawberries.

They say you don't know what you don't know. I didn't know I could make money from fun until 1989, when my company Shari's Bear'ys was born. I'm not bragging when I say it turned out to be a wild success. Well, maybe I am bragging, just a little.

I started as a single woman with a home-based business employing one person—me. The business took off and soon I opened my first retail store in Sacramento. I married Clay a few years later, and the following year our first son was born. The business grew some more, and I was even granted a U.S. patent on my unique strawberry rose bouquet, still a big seller today. I opened a second store and had a second son, then opened a third retail outlet in yet another area of Sacramento. In 1998, in our ninth year, we changed the spelling of our name to Shari's Berries; started the Internet division, Shari's Berries International (or SBI); and opened a 30,000-square-foot production facility. I had a third son this same year. I also gained a business partner, investors, and board of directors. This was fun for a while, but mistakes were made, and the reorganizations that followed were difficult, to put it mildly. In 2006, my heart was broken when the board voted to sell SBI, the Web division, to another company.

But I'm still here! Just ten weeks after SBI was sold, I picked myself up off the floor and started a new company, BerryFactory.com, as an avenue to sell my famous berries online nationwide. And I continue to own and operate my retail locations in Sacramento. I no longer ship the Shari's Berries brand out of the greater Sacramento area.

What a ride it has been. I have to admit it's not always been fun—but it *has* always been interesting. When the hard times come, I remind myself that, as long as you learn something, it's never a mistake.

I was proud of my prestigious title of stockbroker back in the eighties. But that's nothing compared to the pride I have in my famous berries. People love them—and they're not shy about telling me so. Over the years, the famous berries I created have been showcased in Oprah's *O Magazine* and *In Style Magazine (People Magazine)* and on "Wheel of Fortune," "Dr. Phil," "The Apprentice," "The Today Show," HSN, QVC, and the Food Network. A great thrill of my business life was Valentine's Day 2007, when Google modified its Web-site logo so that the second *g* in its logo looked like a chocolate-covered strawberry!

Luxury gourmet-berry gift boxes adorned with my name have shown up at events for the Oscars and the Emmys. When I was a teenager, I dreamed about becoming famous someday, but my dreams were never as fantastic as the reality turned out to be.

But as fun and demanding as my business life has been, it's not the heart of who I am. Who I am first and foremost is a wife and mother. Combining my business and personal lives has not been easy, but here's my secret in a nutshell: always, *always* put your family first. I can work anytime, but I only have one chance to be a good mom. I don't want to wake up someday and find out I missed my sons' childhoods. I don't want my marriage to lose its magic. All the chocolate-dipped strawberries in the world could not make up for that.

My business truly is a family business. My boys have grown up eating new product prototypes—although they complain that I don't bring dipped berries home often enough. (They'd eat them every day if I allowed them to.) They are used to having their mom show up regularly on TV or the radio. They even brag about me to their friends sometimes. Awards don't get much better than that.

But like many women, I often think that if only I had more time, I could be a better mom. I want to give my family 110 percent, while giving my business 110 percent at the same time. It doesn't matter that I know this is impossible—I want it anyway. But I've had to learn that it's okay to be satisfied with 85 percent. We women are good jugglers. That's why we make such great businesspeople.

Many women seem to be interested in my success. My mantra has always been, "If I can do it, anyone can," and this message is hitting home for women. In the last few years, I've been asked to speak at conferences and other large gatherings, especially those tailored to women entrepreneurs. There are women (and men) who have great new ideas and are hungry for some practical knowledge on how to take those ideas and make them real in the world. They want to know how I "did it."

When I first began speaking in front of big audiences, I was a little nervous. Who was I, a small-town girl from Klamath Falls, Oregon, to think I was some kind of authority? What I'd done wasn't that earth-shaking—I'm a berry dipper, for goodness sake!

I've come to see that it's because I'm just a berry dipper that I do have some things of value to share. When I speak, I use index cards, and at the top of the first card, I highlight the words *Greater is He*.

This is from 1 John 4:4: "The Spirit who lives in you is greater than the spirit who lives in the world." This is a verse I love, and it reminds me that God is my helper and I shouldn't be afraid, for He is much greater than any mortal. We all have the opportunity to know the greatness of God through His Holy Spirit, even berry dippers.

My faith and how it allows me to tap into that Holy Spirit is a key to my survival. When I first began speaking, as soon as I saw those words on the top index card, my eyes would fill with tears, and my first few words came out a little choked. I felt like a total dork! So I prayed about it, asking God for help not to cry if He wanted me to continue doing this. I guess He does, because I don't cry anymore (well, not as much anyway).

And so now I've arrived at another "right time" in my life. For years, people have been urging me to write a book about my story, but I've never felt ready. I didn't know the ending yet! And then it hit me—if I waited until I knew the ending, it would be too late, wouldn't it?

So here it is, my story and the lessons I've learned along the way. I'll be sharing some of my closely guarded secrets in these dozen chapters too—the recipe for strawberry pie that began my love affair with strawberries, the lemon pie recipe that's been in my family for generations, the history of Miss Swizzle (our mascot named after our classic drizzled design on top of our strawberries) and how she was born from a mistake, and how to create a party buffet that even teenage boys will appreciate for its beauty—right before they gobble it up.

I want you to have as much fun reading about my life as I am living it. I hope you pick up some pointers along the way, too. Maybe my story can help save some of your precious time. Or maybe it will remind you to have more fun. Maybe this is the right time for you, too.

BERRIED IN
Chocolate

Chapter 1

Do What You Love

I know what a good strawberry is. It seems as if I've always known this. Some people have a sophisticated palate that can pick out a true French pâté or Russian caviar, but my talent is a little more down-home. I just know what makes a good strawberry.

Strawberries have a perfect shape. They look like hearts, complete with a pointy bottom and little dip at the top. We all know what hearts symbolize: love and romance. There's nothing more important than love.

Strawberries are the perfect size for pleasurable eating, naturally bite-sized. You don't have to slice them or dice them, chop them or smash them—although you sure can if you want to, because there's nothing so versatile as a strawberry.

Look at the seeds dotting the strawberry, lined up in perfect symmetry in a repeating V pattern, as amazing as a spider's web. The seeds are tiny enough not to get stuck in your teeth, as raspberry seeds often do. Did you know there's an average of 200 seeds per strawberry? The reason I know this is that I once asked this question on my radio show, and a man called in and said his sons counted the seeds. Now that's dedication. Of course, I was offering a box of gourmet dipped berries as a prize, so they had some big motivation. It just goes to show what people will do for a strawberry.

Nothing is quite as red as a ripe strawberry. You might even say it's the perfect red. Pick up a ripe strawberry warm from the sun, and you can almost see the skin throbbing with the pressure of the red juice within. Bite into that strawberry and your lips and tongue (and if you're not careful, your chin) will glow as if you have just eaten a red popsicle.

Strawberries smell like summer, even in the depths of winter. That's why they are so perfect for Valentine's Day and the winter holidays. We smell that rich scent and it makes us remember lying lazily in the sun, covered with suntan lotion.

But of course the best thing about strawberries is their taste. Have you ever noticed that it is nearly impossible to describe a taste? You have to eat a strawberry to know what it tastes like. But here's a picture of taste: give a toddler his first strawberry. Watch him as his eyes grow big and wide, a grin spreads across his chubby cheeks, and red juice runs down his chin. Even if he can't talk to tell you he likes it, he doesn't have to. You already know.

Admit it; your mouth is watering right now. I hope you have some strawberries in the house. If not, I know where you can get some.

****

Okay, I admit it: I love strawberries. But so do lots of people. Yet not everyone gets to "do" strawberries every day, like me. When I go to work, I get to do something I love. How lucky is that?

I wish everybody could do what they love. Now I know this doesn't always seem possible. There are circumstances and situations where we have to do what we don't even *like* to do, much less love it. But maybe we can all try to do what we love, or at least love what we do. I mean, why else would we have been given a passion, if not to do something with it?

That sounds all fine and grand, but figuring out how to do what you love—and make money at it—isn't always that easy. When I was a little kid, I certainly didn't plan to become the "Strawberry Lady." After all, what kind of a career objective is that?

But looking back, I can see there were many hints.

Playing What You Love

I was a chubby little girl. My mom says you couldn't even see my neck until I was two. My most noticeable feature was my fat little cheeks. I was also a happy kid, always talking (too much, according to my sister) and laughing. And I loved to eat, as long as I got to eat what I liked. Don't get me started on green vegetables. I never liked them, and I never will.

One of my earliest memories is accompanying my dad out to the strawberry patch in our backyard. I was so young that I couldn't pronounce the word "strawberries"; I called them "too-beh-weez." (I had trouble with *R*s and *S*s, so with a name like Shari I was in trouble.) Dad went out to work in the garden, and I went out to eat berries. My mom sent me out with a bucket to fill with strawberries, so she could make strawberry pie. I loved her pies, but the lure of fresh-off-the-vine strawberries was too much to resist. So I developed a simple system: one for the bucket, two for me to eat right then and there.

Why did I like strawberries so much? I guess because they were sweet and beautiful, and they seemed to make people happy when they ate one. I've always liked for everyone around me to be happy. I hate conflict and arguing. And yet, I was always getting into some mischief or other, because of my constant search for fun and more fun.

Another thing I loved was giving gifts, even when I was very small. I liked getting them too, but I liked giving them better. Christmas, therefore, was my favorite holiday. I started planning for Christmas in October. When I was really young, I would make gifts for my family and special friends all by myself, typical childlike things, and then I would spend hours wrapping those silly little gifts in bright and colorful wrappings and ribbons until they were a wonder to behold, at least to my eyes. I kept these gifts stashed under my bed for months, periodically taking them out, gloating over their beauty, and fantasizing about how much people were going to love them.

Christmas Eve was my favorite day of the whole year, because that was when I brought out my gifts from under the bed and put them under the tree. When someone opened his or her gift, I was practically sitting on top of them I was so excited. I've got to say they were kind to me, much kinder than I deserved, since I was such an in-your-face little kid. I was the youngest in the family, with one sister and three stepbrothers, and it must have been tempting for them make fun of my presents. But they didn't. They smiled and said *ooh* and *aah* and made me feel great.

One year, when I was about eight or nine, I had saved up enough money during the year to actually *buy* Christmas presents for everyone. This was a big deal for me. I bought everyone their favorite candy bar. I studied each of my brothers, sister, mom, and dad to make sure I knew which candy bar they liked best. I saved enough of my weekly allowance money to buy one candy bar each week, until I had a candy bar for everyone. I even bought a Giant Tootsie Roll for one of my brothers because he liked them. Yuck! I thought it was a waste of money, but I gritted my teeth and bought it anyway. Then I went crazy with wrapping the candy bars. By the time I got through with those packages, no one could have guessed there was just a candy bar inside.

Even at that young age, I saved my money. I had a feel for money; I liked the way it added up over time. From the time I was so young I couldn't say the word "strawberries," I knew that two for me and one for the bucket was a winning strategy. The bucket was where you put your dreams for tomorrow, and not just your own dreams, but dreams for other people. It always gave me a thrill to put my own money, even if it was just a quarter, into the collection plate at church every Sunday. I'd think of what good things that quarter would buy, and I'd sit in the pew and grin.

When my girlfriend Sharon would come over to my house, one of our favorite things to play was A&W. There was a swimming pool in our backyard, surrounded by a brick barbeque and kitchen area. Sharon and I pretended it was our own A&W restaurant. I cooked fake burgers and poured fake root beer, while she took orders from our imaginary customers and called them out to me. The "customers" raved over my cooking, of course, and gave us big tips. The end of the game was counting out our fake money, which we did quite seriously. This game had everything I liked—giving people what they liked, making good things to eat, and money.

Practicing What You Love

Playing A&W was good training for my first real job, when I was in high school. I worked in a little burger shop—and when I say little, I mean little. It was little even by Klamath Falls standards, basically a box that only two people could fit into at once. I worked the front, taking orders, making drinks, handing over the food, and collecting the money. Maybe not everyone would love this kind of work, but I did. It was playing A&W for real—and making real money too. I could hardly wait to get out of school each day so I could go to work.

To be honest, I loved this job not only because of the work but because it was a popular hangout for some really cute boys. This was where I met my future husband, Clay. He used to come by the burger shop and order chocolate-peanut butter-banana milkshakes from me. He said my milkshakes were the best he'd ever had. I thought he was gorgeous and super cool—four years older than me and with a reputation for giving the best parties in town. I had a reputation as a party girl (it was well deserved—I loved parties), so I figured we were a perfect match.

My next job was a part-time seasonal one, gift wrapping presents at a department store during the holiday season of my senior year in high school. I loved this job too. It was almost as fun as wrapping Christmas presents for my family. We had three different kinds of wrapping paper with matching bows, and strict directions to keep the bows together with the correct paper. After a while, I got bored and decided to mix it up. I didn't ask anyone if I could; I just did it. I like to ask for forgiveness rather than permission, you know? I think of this as pushing the envelope, although I guess some people might say I just like to make mischief. But I *knew* how to wrap gifts. I didn't need or want a list of rules. I always aimed for my packages to be unique, maybe even surprising. The customers loved what I did with those papers and bows. And I loved handing them a sensational package and hearing them say, "Wow!"

Knowing What You Don't Love

Although I loved my gift-wrapping job, especially after I started wrapping the way I wanted to, I still remember an incident that even today makes me cringe. I had just finished wrapping a package with red and white paper and a green bow—*not* the way we were supposed to do it—when the general manager happened to walk through the back, where we were working. She picked up my package and demanded, "Who wrapped this ugly thing?"

I just wilted. I have been accused of being too sensitive, and it is true. If somebody looks at me cross-eyed, I turn into mush. I don't have a tough skin. (This is why I could never be in politics.)

My boss tossed my green-bow package on the table and snapped, "Fix it!" I went home feeling absolutely wrecked. To this day I hate green ribbons and bows. We don't use green ribbon in my company, ever. I don't even like the color green. That extends to green vegetables—I can only eat salad if it's slathered in dressing and cheese—and as for green beans, forget about it. The only exception I can think of is money—I do like greenbacks!

Silliness aside, sometimes it's just as instructive to know what you hate as what you love. I hate argument and conflict. I'll go a long way to avoid them. It's good to know this about myself.

Trying What Others Love

I think what I really wanted when I grew up was to make my mom proud of me. Her approval was what drove me to get good grades, and make first flute in the school orchestra, and win all the prizes I could. I never wanted to hurt Mom's feelings or upset her. Today she says I was a perfect angel, so I guess I succeeded.

Of course, I wasn't a perfect angel. I was just careful not to get caught doing anything she might not approve of. The only time I remember getting in trouble with Mom was when I got home late from a party one night during high school. It was a school night, and I was supposed to be home by ten. The party was at Clay's house, one of his famous parties with lots of popular kids. Oh, I was so madly in love with him, and how could I leave the party to get home by ten, just like a little kid? At ten I called Mom and said I was on my way. At eleven I called and told her the same thing. At twelve I finally headed home. I tiptoed into the house with my shoes off, and there she was sitting on the couch waiting for me. I don't remember what she said. I do remember how she looked at me—and how ashamed I felt for making her upset.

Mom held various jobs outside the home, but I think she was most proud of being a homemaker. Although I admired her, I didn't want to be a homemaker. I did want to be a wife and mom someday, but I wanted to be a rich and famous jet-setting mom, the kind who took my kids with me on trips and stayed at home with them when I felt like it. I wanted to do a lot of volunteer work at my church; throw great parties with lots of phenomenal food, where everyone laughed and had fun, especially me; and have enough money for me and my family so no one had to worry about it—plus enough money to give away.

That money thing was the kicker, of course. My parents weren't poor, but they were a long way from rich. I knew that if I wanted to be "rich and famous" so Mom would be proud, I was going to have to make those riches myself.

The irony is that Mom was always proud of me. If I had told her that I wanted to be a strawberry dipper, she'd have backed me to the hilt. (Well, maybe she would have argued a little.) But there's no way I would have ever planned to own a company that dips strawberries in chocolate. It's funny now to think of all the worrying I did about what to be when I grew up. Really all we have to do is be patient and wait for God's timing in our lives. There is never any need to panic and make bad decisions. But I didn't know that then.

Dreaming of What You Love

My first "real" career dream was of being a stewardess on a major airline, the kind of airline that flew to glamorous places like Paris or New York or Las Vegas. When I was eighteen, I actually got an interview with American Airlines. I had to send in photos along with my application; my mom took them and I looked just like a junior stewardess in my tailored suit. The one thing the photos didn't show was how scared I was when I went up to Seattle for the interview. I was sure this was my destiny, and who wants to fail at their destiny?

I was wrong about it being my destiny, because I wasn't accepted. It was a crushing disappointment, and a blow to my self-esteem as well as my career aspirations. But looking back, I'm glad they didn't want me. I was interested only because it was a way to travel to exciting places. Now that I fly a lot, I know the reality of the job, and it doesn't look that glamorous anymore. Pushing a cart down a cramped aisle and waiting on tired and demanding people would have driven me around the bend—especially nowadays, when flying is practically guaranteed to make people cranky!

Since I wasn't going to be a stewardess after all, I enrolled at Lane Community College in Eugene, just a few hours north of Klamath Falls. Truthfully, I wasn't that excited about going to college. I got good grades in school, all *A*s and *B*s, but education wasn't something my parents pushed on us kids. None of my brothers or my sister went to college; some of them had trouble getting through high school. I basically went to college because I didn't know what else to do with myself. My parents agreed to the deal I put forth—they'd pay my tuition and some living expenses if I moved out of the house. They said okay because after raising five kids all their married life, they could finally be alone!

I had another reason for moving away from Klamath Falls. After going together for nearly two years, Clay had broken up with me, and my heart was in pieces. He wasn't a bad guy; he just wasn't ready to settle down. I tried to understand, but it still hurt a lot. In Klamath Falls everything reminded me of him, and since it was such a small place I was sure to run into him continually. I was looking for a new start and a chance to forget.

So there I was in college, accepting my parents' money and worrying about what I was going to do *now*. I liked selling, making money, giving gifts, and making people smile. Most of all I liked having fun. What I didn't know was how to put those things together. Actually I didn't know you *could* put them together—especially the fun part. It's not as if there was a major in chocolate-dipped strawberries. When I went home to visit, I'd sit in the kitchen with my mom and wonder aloud what I was going to do with my life. I hope I didn't bore her too much.

While in college I worked part time in the same department store where I'd wrapped gifts, only now I had been promoted to a salesperson in the women's clothing department. Since I love clothes, I was good at this. My customers liked me, and I liked helping them look good. The store ran promotions where we could earn special prizes or money for opening up charge accounts, and I nearly always won these promotions. I loved the job, but I knew it wasn't what I wanted to do forever.

Looking for Love in All the Wrong Places

After two years and an associate degree, I left college. One reason was that I still wasn't any closer to figuring out what to do with my life, and school seemed like a waste of time. I wanted to *do* things, not just learn about things.

My oldest stepbrother, Rick, owned a mortgage firm in Southern California, and even though I was only twenty with absolutely no experience, Rick offered me a job as a mortgage broker. When I think now of his belief and trust in a very young and green rookie, I am amazed. But of course, at twenty, we don't think of ourselves as young. And I had complete faith in my ability with numbers and my devotion to hard work. Besides, Rick said I could do it, so it never occurred to me to doubt it.

I did do well as a mortgage broker, in spite of my youth and newness to the industry. Rick was pleased with me, and I was pleased with my prestigious-sounding title and especially the money I was making. It was perfect timing for getting into the mortgage business. Mortgage rates had just plummeted, and everyone was either buying or refinancing. I'd be in the office some nights until after midnight, preparing my loan applications so they'd be on the top of the file for the processor in the morning. I was so busy I couldn't even find time to go to the bank and cash my paychecks.

I was named Rookie of the Year my first year. And it wasn't because I was the boss's sister, either. Rick has a driver personality, and I'm ultra-sensitive, so we clashed at times. But the bigger problem was that I wasn't having much fun. I liked dealing with money, because I was good at that, but there were precious few smiles coming my way. Fun is not a component of the mortgage business.

The most fun I had was hanging out with my sister-in-law Emily, an exceptional cook with her own successful catering business. She liked to have fun, just like me. She taught me how to make homemade holiday gift and food baskets. I made them up for the realtors who were my customers and delivered them personally to the real-estate offices. It was a great way to get business without having to play those "suck-up" games, which never seemed quite right to me.

The baskets included strawberries dipped in chocolate. The realtors went nuts over the baskets, and they especially loved those strawberries. Soon I branched out from Christmas baskets to other holidays or special occasions. I was pretty popular among the realtors, let me tell you. My competitors usually brought them stale doughnuts.

And it didn't just make them happy—it made me happy. When I entered a realtor's office, everybody would get up from their desks and swarm around me. They would be smiling, laughing, and joking around. And I never had to say a single boring mortgage word! It wasn't long before I was delivering berry baskets at least once a month—I didn't wait for holidays anymore. Those baskets were my signature marketing edge. Boy, did they work.

They took a lot of work too. I'd be up until two or three in the morning sometimes, dipping those strawberries in chocolate—and loving it. It was such a release from the stress of the mortgage industry.

But after a few years as a mortgage broker, I still wasn't happy in my job, except when I was making or delivering strawberry baskets. I knew it was time to move on to something different, something more fun.

So where do you go for fun from L.A.? Where else but Mexico? I moved to Puerto Vallarta for five months and sold time-shares on the beach. I played a lot of cards, went out to eat every night, and laughed a lot. It was fun—but not very challenging. So when I got bored, I moved again, this time to Reno, which was closer to home. It was my plan to get a no-brainer job in this glittery town, while I contemplated my next move. I got a job as a photographer for the MGM casino's theater/nightclub, which I thought would be fun. But when I went to my uniform fitting and saw the skimpy short skirt I had to wear, I just couldn't do it. I may have been a girl who loved parties and was a bit of a ham, but I was a modest ham.

So I decided instead to get another prestigious job and make some good money. Again I jumped into an industry I knew little about. This time I became a stockbroker, encouraged by a woman stockbroker I had met who became one of my mentors. I did a crash course, passed my Series 6 and 7 exams, got my license, and was offered a job. I was the only woman and the youngest broker in my office. It was a little lonely—but Clay lived just over the hill in Sacramento!

He had recently moved away from Klamath Falls. I had kept track of him through my sister, Dayna, as they were friends. He had a good job as a swimming-pool contractor. Because we were so close, both away from our small-town roots, it was natural to connect again. I had never lost my feelings for him; no one I'd met in L.A. or Reno ever compared with him. And his feelings for me came back too. We dated back and forth from Reno to Sacramento for about nine months, until we decided our relationship would progress a little faster if we were planted in the same place. So I transferred to my company's Sacramento office.

I thought becoming a stockbroker would be a good move for me. I was good with money and curious about investments, and the title of stockbroker sounds so prestigious! (I was still under twenty-five and impressed by this.) Also I thought you had to work with money in order to make good money.

Well, I did make some money, although not nearly as much as I'd made as a mortgage broker, and my title did impress people. Plus I learned a lot about investments and how the market works. But I quickly learned two other important facts about being a stockbroker. First, it bored me. It wasn't colorful and exciting; it was black and white and drudge and plod. Second, and even more important to me, it was full of rejection. Even your good customers could get nasty if their investments didn't perform the way they wanted. People lose their sense of humor, not to mention their compassion, when dealing with their money. Even worse was trying to get new customers. For example, in the brokerage business, if you make ten phone calls (we called it "dialing for dollars") and only nine of them hang up on you—but one listened—this was supposed to be *good odds!* Considering that it ruins my entire day if someone says one cross word to me . . . well, you can guess that I had too many ruined days.

About the only time I had fun being a stockbroker was when I brought my baskets of chocolate-dipped strawberries, which I'd continued to use as my signature marketing tactic, to the financial classes that my firm held at the local library. When I walked in the door, everyone's face lit up. Word got around about the great treats our financial classes provided, and boy, did the attendance improve.

A big "aha" moment came when our firm moved to a new office and we held a grand-opening party. We had a local caterer come in to do most of the food, but my boss asked me to bring my chocolate-dipped strawberries too. I went all out and made the spread look as beautiful as I could. It was a sensation, far eclipsing anything the professional caterer laid out (and it cost about a tenth as much).

During the party, I had two conversations that had a big effect on me and the rest of my life. My boss came up to me and whispered, "Nobody's talking about anything except your strawberries! It's hard to get them to talk about investments." The room was full of stockbrokers, for goodness sake. Stockbrokers *live* to talk about investments—yet here they were babbling about strawberries.

And then my mentor in the office, a remarkable woman and a highly successful stockbroker, asked me a question. "If you can do this, why are you working here?"

At first I was puzzled. "What do you mean?" I asked.

She said, "You're so good at this, I just wonder why you don't do it for a living."

Click. She flicked a switch in my head, throwing light on an idea I had never even considered before: that it might be possible to make money doing something I enjoyed.

It took a few more months before I acted on this insight, however. I continued to be miserable doing a job I hated, and my job performance started to decline. Soon I had only about two thousand dollars to my name. It was the most broke I'd ever been.

Probably this was part of God's plan for me. Often your courage doesn't show up until it is absolutely necessary.

Doing What You Love Takes Courage

One day I was feeling more stressed than usual. I was sitting in my car, scribbling figures on a legal pad in preparation for a sales call and wishing I could just go home. I looked up and saw a florist delivery van parked nearby. "What a great job that driver has," I thought. "All day long, people are happy to see him. He's surrounded by beauty. When he goes home at night, I bet he feels great."

That florist delivery van was the tiny nudge I needed. I stopped teetering on the edge and leaped. The next day was Friday, and that afternoon I went to my boss and told him I wanted to resign. When he asked why, I informed him that I was going to pursue the idea of dipping strawberries as a full-time business.

He didn't laugh, although I'm sure he wanted to. "Why don't you just take a week off?" he suggested kindly. "Get away and relax."

I don't blame him for thinking I was crazy. From stockbroker to strawberry dipper does sound a bit outrageous. But then, outrageous is my natural style.

I did take part of his advice, though. I took the week off. But I did not relax. Instead I worked on my berry business ideas all weekend. On Monday morning I jumped out of bed at six and ran around the block because energy and excitement were zinging through me. That week I made up sample gift baskets filled with dipped berries and took them to local businesses such as car dealerships and printers. I told them how I had used these baskets to get and keep my real-estate and brokerage clients, and I asked them if they might be interested in sending these gift baskets to their clients.

They certainly were. In fact, I was overwhelmed with great feedback from everywhere I went. My berry business was about to be born.

This time I was a little smarter about leaping. Leaping into an established mortgage business or stockbrokerage is one thing; leaping into a business that is not much more than a hobby is another. I quit my job at the brokerage, and then I took other jobs that would help me learn about the gift delivery business. For instance, I took a job with a balloon bouquet delivery company for five dollars an hour. The low pay didn't bother me, because I loved every minute of that job and learned a lot. And if I loved delivering balloons, how much more would I love making and delivering my beautiful chocolate-dipped strawberries—while making money too?

So in 1989 I started my own gift basket business, working out of my one-bedroom condo and financed by a $1,500 credit-card cash advance. People ask me today if I was scared, but I wasn't. I was too excited to be scared. I owned my own business! Although the first time someone called me an entrepreneur, I wasn't sure I knew what the word meant.

Love Helps You Persevere

It would be great if I could say that my business was all hearts-and-flowers perfection every minute of every day from the very beginning, but no one would believe me—because of course it wasn't. We all know that's not how life works. Although I was having fun and doing what I loved, I was also working my butt off. I was often wiped out at the end of the day, with little energy to put into my relationship with Clay—and I wanted Clay to be my number-one priority. Not only that, but as I learned the business, I made some mistakes that were real doozies! (Luckily I could eat some of them.)

That's why loving what you do and doing what you love is so important. It can keep you going even when you long to stop. I learned this on the first Valentine's Day of my new business.

Since I hadn't been through a Valentine's Day in the gift business yet, I wasn't prepared for the crush of orders I received, even though my boss at the balloon shop had told me you could only make lots of money on Valentine's Day if you were *really* organized. I spent the morning of February 13 doing prep work and last-minute shopping and didn't start putting the orders together until too late in the day.

The phone continued to ring all afternoon, and I ended up with 100 orders to make.

That first year I had one Valentine's Day product offering, a basket filled with one dozen gourmet chocolate-dipped strawberries, with a three-balloon bouquet attached. The gourmet berries were perfect, but that balloon bouquet was a big mistake!

Clay came over that evening after work, and he labored beside me, dipping, arranging, tying ribbons, blowing up balloons—you name it. But at two a.m., he finally gave up. He was out of energy and had to get up at six to go to his own job. So he kissed me goodnight, wished me well, and left me alone—still not done with all the orders.

At 3:30 a.m., a balloon blew up in my face, bruising my cheek and startling me so much that I shrieked. Then I cried out of sheer exhaustion. But I kept dipping, arranging, tying, and blowing. I had no choice.

By the time the friends whom I'd convinced (begged, promised, threatened . . .) to help me showed up at 8:30 a.m. on the fourteenth, I was finally done. My tiny condo was filled with 100 strawberry-filled baskets and 300 balloons. The kitchen was a chocolate-covered disaster. There was a tiny tunnel snaking through the baskets that led from the front door to the bathroom. I crept through the tunnel into the bathroom, closed the door, sat down—and couldn't get myself to stand back up. My stomach hurt from tension, my head was pounding, my cheek hurt where the balloon had burst against it, my fingers hurt from tying ribbons, and my legs and feet hurt from standing. And the worst part of it all was that I still had Valentine's Day *ahead of me.*

Did I still love what I was doing? Not right then. But suddenly I realized that if I gave up, I'd probably never find that love again. If I kept going, I knew it would come back. So I reached deep and found one tiny molecule of energy located in the tip of one of my little toes. And I got on my feet and out the bathroom door.

Then I went gung-ho for another ten hours straight, taking in last-minute orders, dipping and arranging them, blowing up more of those darn balloons, and delivering them to all my new customers. By seven that night I was so tired I could hardly stand, but I insisted that Clay take me out to dinner anyway. First because it *was* Valentine's Day, but mostly because I hadn't eaten in over thirty hours. Now I'm usually very sensitive to looking good. I love clothes and playing with my hair—but not that night. I went just as

I was, chocolate stains, ponytail, and all. I'm sure I was the ugliest Valentine in the place, and I didn't even care.

If you don't have a fire inside, you can get burned out.

Never Stop Loving What You Do

That memorable Valentine's Day was decades ago, and I'm glad to report that the insight that came to me in the bathroom that day was absolutely correct. The love did come back, and that's a good thing, because it was just the first of many all-nighters. I still love what I do; in fact I love it even more. This is my number-one secret of success.

My company was built on chocolate-dipped strawberries. That's pretty simple, and not that special either. There are many other companies that sell dipped fruit products, and some have been doing it a lot longer than I have. What makes us different? Why do our strawberries (and other goodies) seem as if they are covered in pixie dust?

I think it's because we love—really love—making and selling them. Not just me, although it starts with me, but the people who work with me. All day long we're around stuff that looks and smells beautiful. We get to play with our hands and let our imaginations run loose. We are a part of special times in people's lives, such as birthdays, engagements, weddings, and hundreds of other celebrations. Our customers tell us their stories about whom they love and why. We get to share in their happy times.

As a child, I loved giving gifts, especially those I wrapped myself. I loved making things that made people feel good and come back for more. I loved parties and celebrations where people laughed and had fun. When I dreamed of being rich and famous, it was so I could have a party every day if I wanted to. And I loved strawberries because it's darn near impossible to eat a chocolate-covered strawberry and still be grumpy.

That's the real reason I love what I do. What I do thrills people. I help them—and me—have fun. People talk about the bottom line in business, which means the money is what counts. Don't get me wrong—money is important and I like making it and having it. But the bottom line for me is the look on people's faces when they see me or my strawberries coming toward them.

A Berry Good Tip

Many people are confused about how to take their love of baking, or horses, or politics, or bookkeeping, or needlework, or *whatever*, and turn it into a career. I hope my story gives you some ideas in that direction.

But what if you don't know what your passion is? This is true of a lot of us. It was true of me for many years. When we grew up, many of us lost that connection to our true joy. Here's the thing: it's usually not the activity itself that you love but the way it makes you feel. Try this tip and see if it works for you.

Think back to when you were around ten years old. Play detective and ask yourself some questions about you as a ten-year-old, such as: When you went out to play, what did you like to do best? Did you like playing with a gang of friends, or with one special friend, or were you a dreamer who liked to play pretend games all alone? Did you like lots of physical activity? Did you like games with rules and structure? Did you like being on a team? Did you like playing house, or store, or teacher, or movie star? What were your favorite toys? What did you want to be when you grew up?

If you can't remember your childhood, that's okay. Instead, *pretend* that you are ten years old right now. What would you like to play today?

Get in touch with that little kid inside you. She (or he) is still there. What makes her happy? And why?

You're nearly there. If you loved it as a little kid, you still do. Now figure out a way to give her what she wants. I know you can do it.

* * * *

Shari's Secret Recipe #1
Chocolate-Peanut Butter-Banana Milkshake

Made the Old-Fashioned Way

5 tbsp. chocolate syrup
¼ cup creamy peanut butter
1 whole banana, peeled and sliced
1½ cups milk
9 scoops vanilla ice cream (or as many as your blender will hold)

Blend all ingredients in blender until smooth. You can use less milk if desired; the thicker the better. Makes 4 servings.

Hint: Use the very best vanilla ice cream you can find. I prefer Breyers® Vanilla Bean.

Made the Fast and Easy Modern Way

3½ cups vanilla ice cream
2 cups milk
8 frozen chocolate-peanut butter-banana slices from the Berry Factory

Combine ice cream and milk in blender. Drop in dipped fruit and fold into ice-cream mixture by blending on lowest setting. Makes 4 servings.

This is super easy and yummy!

Chapter 2

Look Back to See Ahead

Here is an old lady in her kitchen making a pie, but this isn't your ordinary old lady. Diamond rings sparkle on her fingers as she rolls the dough, and gold bangle bracelets clink merrily on her wrists as she zests the lemons and whips the egg whites. This is Grannie making her famous lemon pie.

On the counter sits an ancient recipe card in Grannie's handwriting. It is stained and faded by now, but that doesn't matter because Grannie never looks at it. She has made this pie a thousand times before.

She makes the crust with lard, not shortening, because that's the way it's done. Lard is what makes it flaky, she says. She never forgets to prick the bottom crust with a fork before baking, so it doesn't puff up in the middle. She pops the crust into the oven to bake while she makes the filling.

Her long red fingernails make a bright contrast against the yellow lemons she rolls between her palms to release their juice. She squeezes the

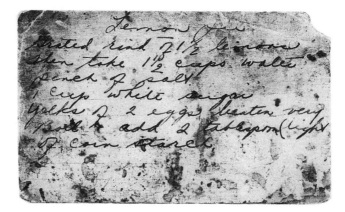

juice into a bowl and then grates the lemon peel. The familiar sharp, sweet smell fills the kitchen. In a saucepan, she simmers water, a cup of sugar, and a pinch of salt, then adds the lemon juice and lemon zest.

While this simmers, she separates three eggs, slimy whites from golden yolks. She sets the whites aside—on the counter and not in the refrigerator—and whisks the yolks slightly. Then she takes a small amount of the lemon mixture and beats it into the yolks. It's important to do this fast so the yolks don't curdle. The diamonds flash and the bracelets tinkle.

She pours the yolks mix into the saucepan with the rest of the lemon mixture and brings the whole thing to a boil, continuing to beat rapidly. She thickens it with cornstarch and water until it is just the right consistency, smooth and creamy, shining with rich and tangy sweetness.

She takes the piecrust out of the oven and sets it off to the side to cool, along with the lemon mixture. Now it is time to make the meringue. She beats the room-temperature egg whites with a little salt until they are a mass of white froth. She adds the sugar one tablespoon at a time, beating furiously between additions, her bracelets clanking against the bowl in a rhythm all their own, a lemon-pie symphony. The meringue gets stiff and glossy as satin, glistening with wet sugar. Miniature mountain peaks form.

Grannie pours the lemon mixture into the cooled crust and slowly and carefully adds the meringue on top, swirling it right to the edge of the crust. With her wooden spoon, she gently arranges the meringue peaks so they look like white waves foaming on a yellow sea. Then she puts the pie back in the oven for just a few minutes and watches it get slowly brown—but not too brown.

And then it is done, removed from the oven by Grannie's still un-wrinkled and glamorous hands. The toasty brown peaks are crowned with tiny dewdrops of sugar that sparkle in the candlelight on the dining-room table. That is where she brings the pie and sets it in the exact middle of the table, the place of honor. Her family waits eagerly, our mouths slightly open in anticipation. We try not to drool.

Have a slice of Grannie's Lemon Pie, sweet and tangy at the same time, just like Grannie herself.

* * * *

Nobody succeeds by herself alone. All of us have had teachers or mentors who have illuminated our paths. It is important to thank these personal guides. Gratitude is good for you! One of the first two-word phrases a baby learns, and one of the first phrases anyone learns in a foreign language, is "thank you." Gratitude is basic everywhere.

I especially appreciate the values I was taught early in my life. I had many teachers who taught me well, but I want to highlight three basic values I learned from two important people: my Grannie Vera and my stepfather, Ben.

Why is it important to think about these basics? Because re-membering my core values helps me stay focused and on course. There are so many ways to slip these days, so many seductions that can make you lose your sense of who you are and what your life means. But when I remember and concentrate on the basic values I learned from these two people whom I loved so much, I know I will not go wrong.

Grannie and Ben were not noticeably alike, so it's ironic that the core values I learned from both of them are the same: work hard, take responsibility for yourself, and have a whole lot of fun.

My Hardworking Grannie

Believe it or not, my grandmother's full name was Veronica Victoria Szymuszkiewiez-Kozaczek. With a name like that, you had to work hard—and you also had to have a sense of humor. Both were true of her.

She was born in Poland (I bet you guessed that) but came to Can-ada as a baby. Her father and mother were farm workers and did well enough so their children always had enough to eat, but not much more than that. The young Vera had to quit school at the age of ten—she got through fifth grade—and go to work as a domestic servant to help support the family. She continued doing domestic work for a long time, even after she met and married my grandfather, also a full-blooded Pole.

Domestic servants work *hard*. Grannie literally spent years on her hands and knees, scrubbing wooden floors in the houses of wealthy people in Winnipeg. By the time she was fifty, her knees were totally shot. But I seldom heard her complain about it. She didn't have time to be bitter—she was too busy working. She was also too busy finding something to laugh about.

Grandpa had a shoe-repair shop in Winnipeg. When he and Grannie moved to Los Angeles, they both worked at a drugstore, Grannie as a telephone operator and Grandpa in the inventory department. She also took care of her children and her own house, and she learned how to cook great Polish dishes from her mother-in-law, Bopcha. Grannie herself became famous in our family for her cabbage rolls and pierogis, Polish potato dumplings, which she'd often cook for the big Sunday meal. She taught her only daughter, my mom, how to cook, too—and we're all glad she did, because my mom is a fantastic cook.

Grannie's hands were never still. If she wasn't cooking or mending, she was cleaning, always cleaning. When I think today of the amount of work she got through in just one day, I have to sit down, which she rarely did.

Watch Those Pennies

I can't say that Grannie loved her work. Instead she loved what it brought her—independence and financial security. Grannie understood that you had to pay for what you had and that you couldn't have more than what you could pay for. She always knew how much money she had and what she spent it on. She wasn't tightfisted; she was just careful.

She and Grandpa were great savers, but they spent their money on what they considered important. They bought a new car every couple of years. They lived in a nice home, but it wasn't extravagant. When Grandpa died in his mid-sixties, Grannie was left comfortably off. She no longer had to worry about money, but that didn't mean she stopped thinking about it. To Grannie, being wasteful was simply wrong.

"Watch your pennies, Shari," she told me many times. "Then you won't have to worry about the dollars. They will be there." I listened to her, because like me, Grannie had a feel for money. She too liked the way it built up over time. This lesson that I learned from her has stuck with me all my life. Never stop overseeing your money. I read somewhere that Oprah still signs every check. Maybe she had a Grannie like mine.

Little Vera

I think Grannie had such a big effect on me because we were so alike. Everyone noticed it—in fact I used to be called "Little Vera." For one thing, I looked just like her. We're the only two in the family with fair skin and blue eyes. My dad is part Eskimo. My sister has his dark hair and eyes, but it would be hard to tell by looking at me that I have Native American blood. Instead I got all the Polish.

Our relationship went much deeper than our looks. After Grandpa died, Grannie came to live near us in Klamath Falls, and I spent a lot of time with her. And after I grew up, even after both she and I moved away from Klamath Falls, we stayed in close touch. We thought alike on just about everything. I could never hide from her—she always knew what was going on with me.

One of Grannie's unique Old Country talents was that she could read tea leaves. She really could! When I was a stockbroker in Reno, I invited my family—Mom, Ben, my sister, Dayna, and Grannie—to visit me. I wasn't very happy in Reno; I was worried about money and had a new job that I was still learning, few friends, and no family around. I was very lonely, but I was trying to hold myself together and forget about how lonely I was. I had a bunch of fun things planned for us to do together, and one of the things we usually did with Grannie was have her read our tea leaves.

Grannie loved to be asked, although we always had to beg a little because her deep Christian faith made her a little uncomfortable about reading the leaves. Finally she said okay, and we made the tea. It works like this. You have to make it the old-fashioned way, with loose tea. You drink as much tea as you can, and then you turn the cup upside down on your saucer and make a wish. The cup sits there until it's your turn. Then you turn the cup right side up and there will be tea leaves adhering to the bottom and sides of the cups. These leaves will form little images, such as a dog or bird, which mean different things, as do their location in the cup. When Grannie read the tea leaves, they told her things about your personality, or things going on in your life at the time, or even what your lucky number was. Of course, it was just for fun, but Grannie was always so darn accurate!

She read Mom's and Dayna's cups first, then came to mine. She picked it up, looked at it, looked at me, and said, "I can't read your cup."

I said, "Huh?"

She set the cup down and said again, "I can't read your cup. You're bottled up tight, stressed out, and unhappy, and that's all I can see."

I was stunned. I had been watching Grannie read tea leaves my whole life, and I'd never heard her say she couldn't read someone's leaves. But she was totally right. I was pretending that whole weekend, pretending that everything was fine and I was happy, and they all bought it—except for Grannie. She could always see right through me, leaves or no leaves.

Grannie was proud of her tea-leaf reading ability, but she looked on it as a fun thing and didn't like to take it too seriously. Sometimes, though, she had some serious results. She spoiled a few surprises, and spilled a few secrets too. One time when she was reading for a new neighbor couple, she saw infidelity in their leaves, which caused an uproar right in her apartment. After that she never read for anyone she didn't know well.

Having fun was important to Grannie. Working hard and saving her money were important because they allowed her to have fun. And her idea of fun was the same as mine—or I guess I should say, mine was the same as hers. I think I might have learned it from her. Or maybe it is in my genes. Why not? I have her hair and eyes, why not her sense of fun too?

Bling, Fast Cars, and Video Poker

Grannie loved to decorate, just like me. Sometimes she made her home a wonderland with flowers, candles, and whatever else she could find to make it special. I remember some of her table settings that took my breath away. One Easter when I was a child, Grannie picked calla lilies out of her yard as a centerpiece for the family dinner table. Using crushed pastel chalks and a wet cotton ball, she dabbed the inside of each lily a different soft color—pink, blue, green, yellow. One Valentine's Day she decorated white candles with red sequins, so when the candles were lit the sequins sparkled red onto the white tablecloth.

Grannie didn't just dress up her table; she liked to decorate herself. She loved her bling, and all those "g" words—glitz, glitter, glamour, and gaudy—applied to her. Well, they apply to me too, because my style is just like hers. The dentist story proves this.

Shortly after Grandpa died, Grandma was window shopping at her favorite jewelry store. She saw this enormous diamond ring and fell in love with it. It is the most amazing ring I've ever seen, about four and a half karats and shaped like a hornet's nest, with a huge diamond on top of a honeycomb of other diamonds. Grannie loved to decorate her hands—she wore her natural fingernails long, and she painted them bright fire-engine red. That diamond ring would look great with her fingernails. However, she thought it cost way too much money. But my mom talked her into buying it, reminding her that Grandpa had left her enough money to enjoy her life. So Grannie bought that ring, the most expensive thing she ever bought, and she wore it everywhere she went. One day she went to the dentist to have her teeth cleaned. The hygienist said, "Oh, your ring is so beautiful." When Grannie thanked her, the hygienist laughed and asked, "Don't you wish it was real?"

"But it *is* real," said Grannie. The hygienist dropped her instruments on the floor.

Now here's the funny part of the story. Many years later, I came home to Klamath Falls for the holidays. Since my family dentist was still there, I decided to have my teeth cleaned while I was home. Well, I had to get ready to go out, didn't I? So I put on a black long-sleeved lacy-knit top with a scoop neck and looped a necklace with large paste "jewels" in different colors and shapes around my neck. I looked good, but my mom took one look at me and burst out laughing. "Shari," she said, "anyone else would wear that outfit for New Year's Eve, and you're wearing it to the dentist!"

Like grandmother, like granddaughter. If you've got to sit in a dentist's chair, you might as well look glamorous while you do.

Grannie left me that diamond ring. She knew I was the only one who would actually wear it and enjoy it and not stuff it into a safety-deposit box. Whenever I have my nails done, I put on that ring and look at my hand—and I can see Grannie's hand right beside mine.

Small-town life in Klamath Falls was really not for Grannie. She and her girlfriends were always taking off for weeklong jaunts to Reno or Las Vegas, and when I was in ninth grade, she and one of her friends finally moved to Vegas. They got an apartment close to the Strip and spent a few years having a wild and glorious time. When her girlfriend had to move back home for financial reasons, Grannie moved in with one of her other friends in Vegas, a woman she actually used to work for as a domestic fifty or sixty years before. They lived right on a golf course. Grannie wasn't into golf, though—she was into gambling. Video poker was her game of choice.

I was living in Los Angeles when I turned twenty-one, and I decided to spend my birthday with Grannie in Vegas. I had just bought a brand-new black Celica, a gorgeous car that I was very proud of. I called her up and said, "Grannie, I'm coming to see you. I just got a new car and I'm driving over." She was thrilled. Before I left I got my nails done in bright red, just for her. On the drive over, a cop pulled me over for speeding. Watching him approach in my rearview mirror, I got nervous and broke one of my new red nails on my gearshift. Plus I got a ticket.

When I told Grannie, she just laughed. She was a fast driver herself. I remember once, when she had a brand-new Cadillac, she took Dayna and me for a ride. We were teenagers at the time. "How fast can it go, Grannie?" we asked, and for an answer she punched it. We went from thirty to ninety in about four seconds. Our heads were flattened against the seatbacks. Grannie was a wild mama sometimes.

We celebrated my twenty-first birthday by playing video poker. I got a royal flush and won $1,000. We laughed so hard and were having so much fun that I kept putting off leaving. It was Sunday night and starting to get dark before I finally left, and I had to drive from Vegas to Los Angeles to be at work on Monday morning.

I had just left Vegas when a bunch of cars started passing me, one after another, as if they were racing. They were all the same make and model, all sleek, black, and new. I thought, "Shoot, my car is black too. Maybe they've got some kind of radar detectors, so if I join them I won't get a ticket. I can get home really fast." I jumped behind the last car and punched it. I went ninety-five miles an hour on cruise control behind all those fast and fancy cars, and I got home in three hours, fifteen minutes. I called Granny, and as soon as she heard I was home, she shrieked, "What? How could you be home already?" She was scared for my safety, but I think she was proud too.

As she got older, into her eighties, she had to move back to Oregon again to be close to my mother. She just wasn't able to live on her own anymore. But I spent a lot of time with her during those years. She'd come to see me in Sacramento. One time I rented a limousine, and we had champagne and got a little giggly while we were driven around. Another time I took her to a spa and we had full-body massages. Oh, I loved to spend money on her, see her face light up, and hear her laugh.

I took her down to Vegas twice a year. She'd see all her friends—there seemed to be hundreds of them—and we'd stay at Sam's Town, which was her favorite place. They still tell stories of her at Sam's Town, like the time she played video poker for about eighteen hours straight. When she finally got tired, she looked at the clock and saw that it was 6:00. She thought it was six at night. But when she went outside, it was morning. That's how much she loved to play video poker.

I threw the mother of all birthday parties for her at her beloved Sam's Town in Las Vegas the year she turned ninety. Everybody who knew her came, lots of them, some from as far away as Winnipeg. For her plane ride to Vegas, I arranged for noisemakers and birthday hats to be given to all the passengers, and the captain toasted her with champagne. I filled her room at the hotel with her favorite red roses. At the party she wore a rhinestone tiara, and we had an Elvis impersonator show up and a cash-stuffed, treasure-chest piñata for her to break. The casino president made a presentation speech, and the giant marquee sign outside the casino wished her a happy ninetieth. I put together a video of her entire life, from Poland to Winnipeg to Los Angeles to Vegas to Klamath Falls, Oregon. It showed all her glamour and glitz and her tea-leaf reading and her backbreaking hard work, and it especially showed her laughing.

I want to be just like her when I am ninety. I think I have a chance.

The Good Stepfather

I believe that divorce is a bad thing, a traumatic experience for a couple and worse for the children. Introducing stepparents and stepsiblings into the mix can be even more painful.

But sometimes it's not the worst thing that can happen. In my case, the pain of my parents' divorce when I was in second grade was made more bearable when a year later my mom married Ben Starr, the amazing man who became my stepfather. I don't like that word, stepfather. It makes him less than what he was to me. He was my second dad.

Ben reinforced the things I learned from Grannie: the value of hard work, the importance of personal responsibility, and how to jump into life with both feet—and have fun doing it. As I told him shortly before he died, if it wasn't for him, I'd still be in Klamath Falls without the strength and confidence to go after the things that I cherish most in my life: my husband, my children, and my thriving business. Ben taught me to be strong, creative, and brave by encouraging my growth at every stage along my path.

Ben was born in a Catholic orphanage in Tucson, Arizona, to a young unwed mother who gave him up at birth. He would never know her. The orphanage was actually called the Stork's Nest. Whenever he was back in Tucson, he would drive by that old building, but not so he could feel bad about his origins. Instead he would marvel at his luck, because Ben's biggest hero, the person he admired more than anyone else, was the woman who adopted him and became his true mother. I never knew her, but she must have been something, because Ben credited her with everything he became. She is the one who taught him about hard work, taking responsibility for yourself, and getting the most enjoyment out of life that you could.

Ben was a hero too, a brave man who didn't think twice about risking his own life to save another. I remember when I first read the newspaper clippings from 1958 when Ben saved a baby from drowning in the canal across from his house. A car had plunged into the canal, and Ben, an experienced diver, jumped in to pull the family out of the car and swim them to the bank. When they were safe, he happened to glance down the canal and spotted a toddler floating away from the wreck, his pudgy little hand waving above the water. Ben jumped in again, got the baby, and gave him CPR until he began breathing again. Everyone lived.

Reading those clippings reinforced my knowledge that Ben was special. It wasn't just me who thought so. But I was luckier than everyone else, because we had a special relationship.

Another Hard-Work Teacher

Ben was the epitome of a self-made man. Money was tight in his family, and he began working when he was still a child. Like Grannie, he had to. And like her, financial security was of first importance—he had seen firsthand how difficult life is without it. It wasn't enough for him to get *by*, he strived to get *ahead*. For most of his adolescence and even into adulthood, he held down several jobs at once in pursuit of getting ahead.

In southern Oregon, the lumber industry is king. When Ben moved there as a teenager, he found a job at a large plywood mill in

Klamath Falls and worked there the rest of his life. His first jobs were mowing the lawns and sweeping the floors. Because of his hard-work ethic and his willingness to do anything that needed doing, through the years he moved steadily upward and ended up as the superintendent of the entire mill. He was the production manager when he met and married my mother. She was also an employee there.

I wish I could say that Ben loved his work, but that would be untrue. Especially as he rose into management, he was often annoyed and frustrated by the political posturing that goes on in any large organization. He wasn't especially "into" lumber or excited by the productivity enhancements that were his job to create and manage. It wasn't a calling to him, it was a job. It paid the bills, supported his family, and allowed him to get ahead so he could do the things he really enjoyed.

However, he did like working with the people in the mill, and as a manager he cared deeply about those who worked for him. Everyone in the mill came to him for advice, about their careers and also about their personal lives. He would listen and dispense practical, no-nonsense words of wisdom laced with humor. He helped people take real steps to improve their situations, and he got them to laugh at themselves. I think this was his true work: guidance. The mill just gave him a place to do it.

When I started my business, I loved to talk with Ben about how to run it efficiently. This didn't mean we always agreed. During my first busy Christmas season in 1990, Ben and Mom came to help me put gift boxes together. Ben's job was to put a couple hundred gift boxes together and fill each one with a berry. We argued for hours about whether he should put all the boxes together first and then fill them or if he should fill each box as he folded it. We finally proved to each other's satisfaction that the most efficient way was to put all the boxes together first before filling them.

He wasn't quite as helpful with marketing and sales. He and Mom came to help with one of my first trade shows. I gave him the job of handing out brochures to people coming by my booth. I told him, "Don't stand in front of the booth, because people won't want to come in to look around. Stand on the side so it's not threatening." He promised to do so, but the soft sell wasn't in his nature. He was more of an in-your-face, upfront kind of guy.

When Mom and I left the booth to grab a quick lunch, Ben was standing on the side, the brochures on a table beside him. By the time we got back, he was right out in front, holding a stack of brochures and thrusting one into the hands of everyone who walked by. "You need to read up on this," he told them.

I had to laugh because he looked so *Ben,* so serious and yet so funny, doing it his own way. Even if he did it wrong (in my opinion, not his), I loved his support. Most of the time he was right.

One of the biggest thrills of my life was when I got to tell him that my annual sales were $250,000, which was a huge number at the time. It made him so proud. That was the year before he died.

The Loveable Tightwad

Ben was another mentor who knew about money. Like Grannie, he was a great saver, and he always knew exactly where his money went. He made sure it didn't go toward anything unnecessary. Take heat, for instance. In our house when I was a kid, the thermostat was never set in the comfort zone. If you were cold in the winter, you put on more clothes. If you were hot in the summer, you'd go swimming. To Ben, utilities were a bad investment. He didn't want to invest money in things that depreciated or disappeared.

Ben was famous for his monthly budgets written on yellow legal pads. Every month he'd start a new page. In his familiar chicken scratch and using a dull pencil, he wrote down what income he expected, including the interest on any investments they had. He recorded each expense, down to the penny. Literally, the penny—Ben did not believe in rounding up or down. He nickel and dimed my mom to death that way; it was one of the few complaints she had about him. It was her job to handle the household—groceries and miscellaneous expenses—on the allowance Ben gave her each month. She was a little crabby the first day of the month when she had to balance the checkbook.

Ben didn't formally teach me, or any of us kids, how to manage our money. But we all learned by watching him manage his. I have always lived well below my means, and I don't suppose I'm going to change now. I enjoy making a dollar stretch. I clip coupons. My kids joke that we can't go out for pizza unless I have a coupon. I also make lists on legal pads, although mine are white, not yellow. I write down my daily to-do list and any stray ideas that might pop into my head. I love crossing off items. I got this from Ben.

For Ben, managing your money and your time was what you did

as a responsible adult. We always knew, even when we were young children, that he did not intend to support us forever. He expected us to grow up and support ourselves. We all knew we had to move out after we graduated from high school, unless we had a job and paid rent or went to college. That was it, period. Every one of us kids got the same high school graduation present: a set of new luggage. It wasn't a subtle hint. "Don't let the door hit you on your way out," Ben said. As the youngest of the five kids, I saw that he meant what he said. The other four took the luggage and moved out the summer after they graduated. They didn't have a choice. So by ninth grade I was already thinking of what I wanted to do with my life. I knew I didn't have a lot of time to figure it out.

He was just as forceful when it came to teaching us to manage our time. If he said he'd pick us up from the movies at 4:00, we knew we'd better be there by 3:50, because ten minutes early meant "on time" to him. He taught us that being punctual was a responsibility we owed to others. Nobody has a right to steal time away from someone else. Time is money, you know.

Tough Hide, Soft Heart

I don't want to make Ben seem like some kind of humorless cop, because he wasn't. I think he had to put on such a tough exterior sometimes because his heart was too tender. He loved my mom; he loved his sons; he loved his stepdaughters, whom he thought of as his daughters. He loved his employees and his friends. And he showed his affection. If you came to him with a problem, it became his problem.

When I was in junior high, we had a family dog. The dog was half-poodle and half-wiener dog, so Mom named him Weenie-Poo. He was a funny-looking dog with some strange habits. Ben loved him. He took him on vacation, took naps with him, and of course loved to make fun of his name. One night Weenie-Poo was run over by a car and killed on the highway. A neighbor called to tell us, and Ben went down to get him. He brought Weenie-Poo's body home and buried him on the hill in front of our house. It was a cold dark night, so he shone the car headlights on the hill so he could see what he was doing. From the window, Mom and I watched and cried. Afterward the three of us sat on the couch with Ben in the middle. Mom cried as she leaned her head on his shoulder. I cried as I lay my head in his lap. Ben hugged Mom and stroked my hair, but he didn't cry.

At least he didn't cry right then. About two days later, Mom found Ben sitting in the bathroom crying. "Ben, what's wrong?" she asked. All Ben could say was, "My dog."

He wanted to seem tough, but we all knew he wasn't. Tough guys have no room for tenderness. Ben was strong. There's a difference.

Spend Your Time and Money Wisely—on Fun

Ben meticulously monitored every dollar in pursuit of that same goal he'd had all his life—to get ahead. When he was ahead far enough, he was going to retire and have fun all the time. He had it all figured out—his goal was to retire before he was sixty. When he was in his mid-fifties, his boss retired and Ben was offered his job as general manager of the whole mill. It meant a much bigger salary and stock options. He turned it down. He had his plans all written down on his yellow pads, and he knew he'd be able to retire anyway in less than five years, with his goal of a million dollars saved. "Why do I need any more stress?" he asked. "Fun is not part of the general manager's job."

He retired at fifty-nine, with his million dollars in retirement money safely invested. At sixty-one, he was dead of prostate cancer.

That's why I am so glad he never postponed having fun, even while he was working his butt off. He didn't mind spending money, as long as it was for something worthwhile—and for Ben, enjoying life was worthwhile.

A few years after Ben and Mom got married, when I was in sixth grade, Ben took the whole family to Hawaii. He had planned for it all year (you can bet it was written down on his yellow legal pad). We went first class all the way, staying at the finest hotels and traveling in limousines. We stayed for two weeks and visited three islands. We went to the fern grotto on Kauai, the black sands and Mauna Loa on the Big Island, and Diamond Head and Waikiki Beach in Honolulu. It was a magical trip and nobody wanted to leave. Dayna and I begged Ben, "We don't want to go home. Please can we stay for just a few more days?" He just shook his head. But later that day, when Mom and Dayna and I were out shopping, Ben went out and found a travel agent. He made arrangements for us to spend three more nights, switching our flights and hotels. When we got back from shopping he surprised us with the news. That still ranks as one of the best surprises I ever got.

Another time, just before Christmas one year when I was a teenager, Ben called everyone into the living room. He said, "Okay, everyone, line up. I want your mom to take our picture." So we shrugged and lined up, and Mom took a picture of us standing there in front of the Christmas tree. Then he said, "Oh wait, I forgot something. We have to take another picture." And he handed each of us a brand-new, crisp, $100 bill. We all said, "Wow!" and Mom took a photo of us looking really happy. Then Ben said, "Now go pack. We're going to Vegas!"

And we did, first class again all the way. Just like Grannie, Ben loved Las Vegas. He loved Grannie too. He took us all, including Grannie, to Vegas to celebrate her sixtieth birthday. Now that was a wild time. When Ben spent money, he spent it the right way.

He used his money to broaden my horizons, too. In 1979 he put up $4,000, a lot of money then, for me to go to the Philippines as an exchange student. When I got married years later, he and Mom gave Clay and me another $4,000 for our wedding and honeymoon expenses. Plus he is the one who counseled me to buy an extravagant wedding dress. I had fallen in love with a "dream dress" that cost $1,200. That was *way* over my budget, and certainly our simple wedding did not require an elaborate dress. But when Ben found out that I wasn't going to buy the dress I loved, he told me, "Shari, there's a time to be frugal. This is not the time." I bought the dress and I felt beautiful. I've never regretted it.

I've always felt that Ben and I had a special relationship. Of course, my sister and brothers felt that they had special relationships with him too. I guess he made all of us feel special. But I was the one he loved to tease, maybe because I nearly always fell for his jokes. I remember a Christmas present he gave me. I've mentioned that I hate green vegetables. Green beans are the worst ever. I hate them; I don't even like to look at them. When I was a kid, my parents insisted I eat some vegetables. I remember sitting at the dinner table, watching my three green beans get cold. (Three was the amount of beans I was required to eat.) Eventually I learned how to swallow a green bean whole, as if it was a pill. It was the only way

I could get them down. (It still is—only now I don't force myself to eat them.) Anyway, one Christmas there was a giant gift for me under the tree. It was bigger than a basketball, rounded, and very heavy. When I opened it, I found that Ben had bought one of those huge industrial-sized cans of green beans, enough to feed an army platoon. That was his gift to me that year. At the sight of my face he laughed so hard he cried.

Because Mom, Grannie, Dayna, and I were Polish (Dayna and I were only half), Ben told us a lot of Polish jokes. He sort of collected them. One of his favorites was one he made up himself. Right after he married Mom, someone at work asked him, "Hey, Ben— know any new Polack jokes?" "Yes!" Ben replied. "Three of them just moved in with me."

Ben loved Grannie (she loved him too), and he also liked to tease her. One time he went on a business trip to Dallas. Grannie lived in Vegas at the time and had planned a trip to Oregon to visit us. Ben arranged to fly home the same day as Grannie was flying in, and he made elaborate arrangements with a travel agent to make sure they were on the same flight and seated in the same row. He told Mom what he was doing but told her to keep it secret from Grannie.

At the time, Ben had grown a big beard and was wearing his hair long. He liked to change his appearance whenever the mood struck him, and you could never predict how he'd be wearing his hair, or how he'd be dressed, or if he had facial hair or not. He just liked to mix it up for fun. Since Grannie hadn't seen him for a while, she didn't know about the beard. Ben was a big burly guy, so with his beard he looked like Grizzly Adams. The outsized cowboy hat and boots he bought in Texas, just for this charade, made him even more unrecognizable.

On the plane, Grannie was on the aisle and Ben at the window, with a stranger between them. Grannie obviously didn't recognize him. After they got up in the air, Ben whispered to the lady sitting next to him, "That's my mother-in-law next to you. She doesn't recognize me. Will you help me mess with her?" The lady went along with the joke, and she and Ben had a great time saying outrageous things to each other during the flight, with Grannie listening and wondering how she could get away from these nuts.

Near the end of the flight, Ben took off his hat, pushed back his hair, leaned over, and smiled at Grannie. That's when she recognized him. She shrieked, "Ben!" and punched him right in the chest. Then she laughed. What a pair they were.

Shortly before he retired, Ben made one of his fun dreams come true. He thought it would be fun to travel the West on a motorcycle, with Mom on the back and their hair streaming behind them from under their helmets. So he bought a huge golden-winged Honda traveling bike with all the biker trimmings. For their vacation that year, he and Mom did a loop through Vegas and L.A. to Tucson, where Ben was born. From what I hear, it was a glorious trip. It was so much fun that they bought a mini-motor home and went on mini-vacations. They planned to buy a big motor home when he retired and just travel throughout the country, making their snowbird base in Ben's beloved Tucson.

The retirement was short. They lived in Tucson just one season before Ben was diagnosed with cancer, and they returned to Oregon to be with family while he fought for his life.

He lost. Ben died at home, with a view of majestic Mt. Shasta framed in his bedroom window. We were all there with him.

It's Not About How Long You Have

Grannie lived until she was ninety-three. Ben died when he was only sixty-one. But I don't think it matters how much time we have. It only matters how we use that time. Both Grannie and Ben used their time to the fullest. They worked hard, they played hard, and they took care of their own. They really lived while they were alive, and the lessons they taught me still live on, in me.

Now it's my turn to live my life to the fullest, and take those lessons I learned from Ben and Grannie and pass them on to my children, my friends, my co-workers, and anyone else my life happens to touch. Because you are reading this book, that includes you.

Work hard, take responsibility for yourself, and most of all, have fun.

A Berry Good Tip

In Proverbs 3:13-14, the Bible says, "Happy is the person who finds wisdom and gains understanding. For the profit of wisdom is better than silver, and her wages are better than gold." Who were the mentors and teachers who helped you gain wisdom? Who taught you the basic values you live your life by? The basics are important. They are the foundation for everything else.

Have you thanked those people? Have you given them credit for the ideas they shared with you or the support they gave you? If not, thank them now. If you've already thanked them, thank them again. Expressing gratitude pays huge dividends.

And, of course, learning never ends, and teachers continually appear in your life. Don't be too proud to listen and learn. For instance, when Ben kept telling me I should do more marketing for Father's Day, I told him he didn't know what he was talking about. "Father's Day is just not a big holiday," I explained. "Nobody is going to buy fancy strawberries for their dad. They're a girly thing." Ben told me I was wrong. "If you marketed them right, they would sell," he said. But it wasn't until after Ben died that I started marketing Tuxedo Berries, strawberries wearing "tuxedos" made of white and dark chocolate. I thought I'd do it just once, for the first Father's Day after Ben died, in his honor. But they sold so well we are still doing them every Father's Day. He was right all along.

So whether it's for your business or your personal life, don't be afraid to ask for people's ideas and suggestions. You don't have to take the advice, but it's a really good idea to at least listen with an open mind.

And always remember to thank them. Give them the credit they deserve.

* * * *

Shari's Secret Recipe #2
Grannie's Lemon Pie

Piecrust

1 cup flour
½ tsp. salt
3 tbsp. oil
3 tbsp. butter-flavored Crisco (tip: use a ⅓ cup measuring cup, fill it half full with Crisco, then top it off with the oil)
2½ tbsp. cold water

Lemon Filling

3 egg yolks
1½ ripe lemons
1½ cups water
Pinch of salt
1 cup sugar
6 tbsp. cornstarch

Meringue

3 egg whites
¼ tsp. salt
6 tbsp. sugar

For Piecrust: Preheat oven to 425 degrees. Mix all ingredients for piecrust in a medium-sized bowl. I start off with a big fork, then use my fingers to blend with. This is faster and easier, but be sure to have 2 sheets wax paper and a rolling pin all ready to go. Roll out crust between wax paper, line pie plate, and *be sure* to prick the bottom and sides of crust thoroughly with fork. Bake piecrust at 375 degrees for 10 minutes or until golden brown. Set on rack to cool. (This is actually my other grandmother's piecrust recipe—Grandma Bellon, my dad's mother. She was a great cook and an amazing pie maker. This is a "hardy" crust, definitely not a fancy thin style. When Grandma passed away, one of her treasures that I inherited was her rolling pin, the one item I wanted the *most*.)

For Lemon Filling: Take eggs out of the refrigerator and let them sit for an hour or so, until they are at room temperature. (This will make the eggs in the meringue whip fluffier.) Roll the lemons with the palms of your hands to release the juice. Squeeze ½ cup juice into a cup. Then take a zester and grate about 1 tbsp. lemon peel. Pour the water into a saucepan. Add salt and sugar, and bring mixture to a simmer. While waiting for the water to get hot, separate the eggs. Slightly beat the egg yolks in a small bowl. (Save the egg whites for the meringue.) Then add the lemon juice and the grated lemon peel to the saucepan of water. Take a small amount of the lemon mixture and beat into the beaten egg yolks, beating quickly so they don't curdle. Then pour this back into the saucepan, beating rapidly. Bring to a boil. Mix together a small amount of water with the cornstarch. Add to the lemon mixture, stirring constantly until thickened. Cool the mixture slightly and pour it into the baked pie shell.

For Meringue: In a medium-sized bowl, beat egg whites and salt until frothy. Add sugar, 1 tbsp. at a time. Beat continuously until the meringue is stiff and glossy. The meringue is ready when it can hold a point yet still looks moist.

Gently pour the meringue on top of the lemon filling, carefully swirling to the edge of the piecrust. Bake at 350 degrees for 12 to 15 minutes, checking frequently so the meringue does not get too brown.

Chapter 3

Find Your Talent

It's me, little Shari, picking strawberries in the backyard strawberry patch and dreaming of the strawberry pie my mom will make from these berries—the ones I don't eat right now. My mom is magic. As wonderful as these strawberries are, warm from the vine, my mom knows how to make them taste even better.

When I bring my bucket into the kitchen, my mom looks inside and tells me I am the best berry picker she has ever seen. She washes the berries in water to get the dirt off, although when I eat them off the vine the dirt doesn't bother me at all.

She gets a bunch of graham crackers and crumbles them into a bowl. She adds sugar and melted butter and mixes it up. It looks like light brown mud. Then she spreads butter in her glass pie pans and presses the crumb stuff all around the edges and bottoms of the pans. Sometimes she lets me press it down too, if I wash my hands first. We have made the crusts. They go into the fridge to wait until we have the strawberry filling ready.

The strawberry filling is my favorite part. First Mom gets about a cup of the strawberries and puts them in a pan. Then she mashes them with her potato masher. I can help with this if she wants. The strawberries get all soft and goopy. They smell great. Then Mom adds sugar and corn-starch to the goopy strawberries and puts the mixture on the stove. She has to stir it constantly until it boils. Then she takes it off the stove and adds four drops of red food coloring. Now it's starting to get all shiny. Mom tells me this is called the glaze.

We put the glaze in the fridge to get cool. Mom lets me lick the spatula she stirred the glaze with. Yum. Mom laughs at me because I have a big red mustache.

We take the glaze out of the fridge and dump all the rest of the strawberries into it. Mom washes the spatula that I licked and uses it to toss the berries gently until they are all coated with the glaze. She pours the strawberries and glaze into the graham-cracker crusts and puts the pies back in the fridge. They are almost ready to eat. Mom says they have to "set."

I don't like the "set" part because I want to eat my pie right now. One of the pies is just for me. Mom used to make only one pie, but I was scared I wouldn't get my share. I'm the baby of the family, you see. But now that Mom makes two pies, I don't worry.

Finally we get to eat the pie. The others in my family like to put whipped cream or Cool Whip on the top of their pie, but I don't. I don't want a white pie. I like my pie red and shiny and strawberry tasting.

My mom can make strawberries into magic. She is the best artist I know.

****

I come from an artistic family. My mom's family contains commercial artists, still-life artists, sign painters, jewelry designers, and engravers. My mom is super talented herself, although she refuses to call herself an artist. When Dayna and I were little girls, she drew, freehand, a flower garden on the walls of our bedroom and painted the flowers yellow and pink and red. No boring wallpaper for my mom! In the 1970s, she took one class in ceramics and in no time was so advanced she opened her own ceramics shop, called the Greenware Factory, where she poured greenware and taught classes. Just recently she painted an entire *Star Wars* theme on my son Max's bedroom ceiling and walls. She designs and paints a line of decorative plates and wine bottles. And, of course, she is the artist who designed my business's first logo, back when it was still Shari's Bear'ys, which is a name she dreamed up. On the wall of my first store, she painted a six-foot lady bear dressed in a maid's uniform, holding a basket of berries.

My son Hogan has evidently inherited his grandmother's talent, because he too loves to draw, and his clever cartoons have been decorating our refrigerator for years. He took a college class in cartooning when he was only thirteen and aced it.

But me? Not so much. I never thought of myself as a creative person. I can't draw (not even stick figures), can't write poetry, can't sing, can't act, can't even model—I'm too short and curvy. I love giving parties, dressing up, and decorating, and I have to admit I am a natural-born ham. One year I took my employees out to celebrate at a fancy Italian restaurant, where I got up on stage dressed as a big, ugly cowboy with my teeth blacked out, a beer belly, and chew in my back pocket, singing Trace Adkins' *One Hot Mama*. Believe me, no one would have called me talented that night.

Creativity Has Many Faces

In spite of my lack of artistic leanings, eventually it dawned on me that my passion for product innovation and marketing, my primary talents, can also be called creative, even artistic. In fact, I am listed as an *Inventor* at the U.S. Patent Office, for my creation of our signature product—long-stemmed strawberry "roses" packaged to look just like the real thing, only mine are edible! And what could be more creative than an inventor? My talent is thinking of over-the-top, one-of-a-kind edible gifts, and using this talent has enabled me to transform a chocolate-dipped strawberry into one of America's most popular gift choices. I like to say I now *own* Valentine's Day, nationwide. Okay, maybe that's a little overstated, but it's close.

I've been called the "Queen of Marketing and PR," and I have to admit that I like being the queen. I'm constantly thinking of new ideas. It's always on my mind, because I live my berry business. My love of marketing makes it easy for me to create new marketing venues or take advantage of opportunities that seem to pop up frequently if you're on the lookout for them. I'm always thinking of how I can get my products in front of someone or help them remember my company when they are wondering what to get someone as a gift. Everyone is my potential customer, and I never let myself forget that. I bring my brochures and business cards with me wherever I go—in fact, no person in business should *ever* be caught without a business card. It's the number-one rule!

But pushing the same things over and over would get boring—both to me and to my customers. You have to keep your products new and different and exciting. I don't want people to get bored with shopping at my company. Of course, I will always offer the traditional one-dozen gift box, because some people love the tried and true, but others wonder how many times you can send your wife (or husband, girlfriend, secretary, boss, friend, customer, etc.) the same one dozen dipped strawberries.

I think of my business as an alternative to the florist. I create a mood, not only with the products, but with the packaging. How about a chocolate-dipped wine bottle or a silver-plated jewelry box with chocolate candies within? How about strawberries and chocolate coins spilling out of a treasure chest, or berries dipped in white chocolate dyed pink for Breast Cancer Awareness Month? How about chocolate-dipped CD cases? Yes, we have done all of these.

Thinking of new products and ways to package those products enables me to let loose my flair for glitz, glitter, big bold colors, and eye-catching designs. It's so much fun! Over the years, our new products, many of which are still offered, have included:

Baseball Berries™: Berries dipped in white chocolate and adorned with edible red stitching. I love baseball and many sports!

Jelly Belly® Berries: Strawberries dipped in white, dark, or milk chocolate and sprinkled with Jelly Belly® beans in flavors of coconut, peanut butter, strawberry cheesecake, and more.

Chocolate-Dipped Grape Clusters: A pound of red seedless grapes, still on the vine, dipped in dark, milk, or white chocolate and dusted with an edible golden powder.

Berry Blossoms: A dozen luscious, fancy, dipped strawberries presented in a long gold rose box and nestled among rose vines, then tied off with a large gorgeous bow. They are just like sending flowers and candy at the same time!

Berry Bobs: Small berries slid onto a skewer and the entire stick dipped into chocolate. It had always been a challenge to find a way to sell berries that were too small to qualify as our premium berries. But it's terrible to waste perfectly good tasting strawberries just because they're a little small, and this idea was perfect—it made good economic sense and artistic sense too!

Various Berry Offerings for Men: A football wicker basket with two berries, a small beer, and two pretzels all dipped in chocolate; a black top hat filled with "tuxedo"-style chocolate-dipped strawberries; a replica of a turn-of-the-century produce truck with two berries in the bed. I learned that strawberries and chocolate are not just for girls. Boys like them too.

Oh, I could go on and on and never really be done, because I'm always thinking of new ways to dress up a strawberry—or anything else. I didn't even mention peanut butter berries, chocolate-dipped frozen bananas, cheesecake berries, sugar-free chocolate-dipped berries—I must stop! See how fun this is?

It's not only fun, it's art. After I recognized my marketing ability for what it was, a creative talent, I was able to find ways to foster it, both in myself and in others. I'm often asked where I get my ideas, and I'd like to share how I think this works for me, in hopes that you will find and encourage your own creativity. I promise you have it—we all do.

Listen to Others

Many of my best new product ideas have come directly from my customers. We had a bride come in and tell us she didn't want a traditional cake at her wedding—could we make something out of strawberries and chocolate instead? You should have seen the three-tiered wonder we came up with. We arranged hundreds of dipped and decorated strawberries in cascades of glory. It is now a standard product offering, just for weddings.

How we created the cake was based on the way bakeries make fake cakes for their window displays. Those aren't real cakes in the windows; they're usually Styrofoam rounds with frosting and decoration. We take the Styrofoam rounds and wrap them in colored Mylar wrap that matches the bride's colors, usually silver or gold with her accent color. Between the tiers are three plastic pillars where we put the berries. We take a hundred strawberries on toothpicks and stick them all over the pillars. You can't see the toothpicks. The guests just pull the berries off and eat them. On the very top of the cake are two especially large dipped berries, one a bride-styled berry (a berry dipped in white chocolate with white lacy drizzle and a pink chocolate pearl necklace) and the other a groom-styled berry (a berry wearing a dark and white chocolate tuxedo). Instead of the traditional cutting of the cake, the bride and groom pull off their special berries and feed them to each other. It is so cool!

Even my patented strawberry-rose bouquet was based on a suggestion from a customer. He had sent his wife a dozen dipped strawberries in a willow basket, and she loved them. Then he asked us, "What else do you have? Do you have something like flowers?" Great idea! The strawberry-rose bouquet was born, and now my customers get the beauty of the flowers and the sentiment behind them—plus they can *eat* them! Women often complain that flowers die too quickly. But with my flowers they can wear them around their hips for a much longer time.

Speaking of hips, our line of sugar-free dipped berries was developed because of the increasing number of requests we got from diabetics and low-carb dieters. If you get a request for something more than two or three times, and you don't have it, then you'd better develop it. I always listen to my customers. They're not always right, though, no matter what that slogan says. Sometimes their ideas aren't so good. But so what? It costs nothing to listen, and the payoff can be great.

I often pretend that I am the customer. There's this girl named Shari out there, and she has this life that includes family, friends, hobbies, a job, and so on. What kinds of gifts does she want to give that we don't yet offer? What does she wish we made? How can we make her gift giving more convenient? Where is she going to use this product? What does it look like? Why is it appealing?

I ask my employees (and my friends and family) to share their product or packaging ideas with me. I always listen, and I *never* put down or make fun of their ideas. (Even when they are funny. With three boys at home, you can bet I hear some funny—sometimes gross—ideas.) I'm willing to put my money where my mouth is, too. When an employee gives me a new idea that we use, they get a fifty-dollar bonus.

Another source of new ideas—new to me, anyway—is other businesspeople who sell similar products. When I met Debbi Fields, the founder of Mrs. Fields' Cookies, she told me that whenever she flew she passed out samples of her cookies to the other passengers. I thought, "I can do that!" So the next time I flew, I took 150 dipped strawberries with me on a flight to Las Vegas and gave them to the flight attendants to pass out to the passengers. I guess you could say I owned that plane. The next week I had to fly to New York, and this time I brought 350 dipped strawberries with me. This was even better—I mentioned to the flight attendant that my first dream was to have her job, and before I knew it, I was upgraded to first class and given a flight attendant's apron and aisle cart and shown how to use it, and I got to deliver my berries personally to the flight crew and passengers. Everyone raved about them, of course. What a great marketing concept. Now I take product samples with me whenever I fly. The goodwill it buys me is beyond price. Those berries may be free at first, but once people taste them, I know they'll come back for more and probably become customers for life.

Pay Attention

New ideas are everywhere—all you have to do is pay attention. When people ask me for the "secret of my success," I tell them that I am always on the alert for things that will benefit my business. That doesn't mean I work myself into the ground. It just means that I know new opportunities will show up at any time, and if I want to take advantage of them, I need to recognize them when they appear.

I'm a typical woman because I love to shop. Whenever I'm out shopping, I'm always looking at merchandise and thinking: Could we put berries in that and sell it? Would a berry fit in that? Could we ship that with a box of berries? How would that taste dipped in chocolate?

I'm fortunate because my business is ideally suited to any kind of gathering. Life is full of opportunities to party. Weddings, anniversaries, graduations, birthdays, and holidays—I market for them all. The only gathering I don't market to is funerals, although I've taken dipped strawberries to those too, and they are always appreciated.

But if I had stopped there, I would not be as successful as I am. My trademarked baseball berries, for instance, were inspired by a sponsorship I did with Sacramento's River Cats baseball team, which is the farm team for the Oakland As. They took off in a big way.

Needs inspire creativity. After 9/11, America was swept by a huge wave of patriotism, and we had customers calling up and wanting something red, white, and blue. I had a vision of a white strawberry with a blue star and red stripes going sideways across it. We called them our Star-Spangled Berries and sold many thousands of them for July 4, 2002.

One of my earliest creative marketing ideas was to send a free box of berries with a personal note from me to every famous person with the name of Barry or Berry. I don't know how many we sent, or how many responded, but I do know one who did: Halle Berry. I got a note of thanks back from her assistant, who was interested in my products and my story. Halle became a great customer, often ordering boxes of berries to send to her friends and family. On Oscar night 2002, we were all rooting for her to win Best Actress for *Monster's Ball*. When she did, she sent my berries to everyone she knew! And there were plenty of big names among them. That free box of berries brought me more publicity than I could ever have imagined.

My mind is always working, looking for new ideas. I don't always look for them consciously—I trust that they will come to me. So far they always have, and not just for my business, but in all aspects of my life. When we moved to a new house with more space, I kept the front room empty. Not only does it give the boys a place to throw balls inside the house, it allows room for new decorating ideas to come into play, before I spend money on making them real.

Clearing the mind often leads to different ideas. Some of my most creative ideas have come to me while I sleep. I keep a notepad on my nightstand because I often wake up in the dead of night with a new idea sparkling in my brain. I've found that if I write it down on my notepad I'll go right back to sleep, secure that I've captured that idea. Many of these ideas are actually good ones.

One Saturday night, I had a dream about decorating wine glasses and champagne glasses with chocolate to go with our chocolate-dipped wine and champagne. I woke up Sunday morning with this cool visual in my head. I went down to the shop to do it to see if it worked. It did.

Outside That Box

Speaking of chocolate-dipped wine bottles, that was a creative idea that illustrates the cliché "think outside the box." The saying may be trite, but it is still true. Sometimes good ideas are hidden in the common things around you, but you're not looking at those things in a new and different way. Shift your perspective, just a little, and new ideas may ripen like strawberries in summer.

I love chocolate and I love wine. Wine and chocolate go together, don't they? They both make luscious gifts because they smack of luxury and indulgence. Yet who ever heard of them actually combined?

How would you do that? Not chocolate wine, but . . . how about a wine bottle dipped in chocolate?

Yes, but how would you drink it? Wouldn't your hands become a chocolate mess while pouring? Which wine would complement chocolate best? How could I package this combination?

All these questions were answered when we found, through much trial and error, a way to create a chocolate-dipped bottle of wine. I chose a blend of Zinfandel and Petit Syrah, which goes well with chocolate. The bottles are first shrink wrapped to keep them sanitary and then tilted and lowered by hand into warm, melted chocolate, a special formula based on Guittard chocolate. After that, more chocolate is drizzled over the coating in reverse colors.

Even more novel is the way we package the wine. It's got a zipper! Well, sort of—really it's an embedded pull string that peels the chocolate from the bottle all at once, so you can eat the chocolate while drinking the wine. And there's a decorative cellophane wrap on the outside that keeps your hands clean.

The idea of chocolate-dipped wine is so unusual that people always ask me the same questions I asked myself when I was trying to develop it. How do they eat the chocolate off the bottle? I show them there are instructions and a pull tab that will unzip the chocolate, but sometimes they're still confused. One woman asked, "Can I lick it off the bottle?" I said, "You can eat it any way you want."

Our wine has been so successful that in its first year we won a Double Gold Award at the El Dorado County Fair. El Dorado is a Zinfandel appellation, and there was very stiff competition. Double Gold means "best of the best." Wow! But one of my favorite compliments came from a customer who said, "I love this—you can wake up with a cavity and a hangover at the same time!" (Just kidding. Drink in moderation, and always remember to brush your teeth!)

Another example of looking at things in a new way is the Caramel Apple Wedgies™. You think you know what wedgies are, don't you? But you're probably not thinking about *my* wedgies.

I have revolutionized the caramel apple. I've always loved them, but they are big and messy and hard to eat. By the time you eat a caramel apple you are sticky all over—or your kid is. I thought, "Why not make an individual slice of caramel apple?" So we took a wedge of a tart Granny Smith apple, wrapped it in caramel, and dipped it in chocolate. Sometimes we sprinkle nuts on top, and the one we dip in white chocolate has cinnamon sprinkled on top. Yum.

Then I thought, "What can we name this creation?" Names are very important. They are the first major step in marketing. My son Hogan, who was thirteen at the time and a natural-born marketing whiz who just might take over the business one day, said, "Mom, I have the perfect name for your new apple product. Call them Wedgies! It'll be the best wedgie they've ever had!"

I loved it! We took the product and Hogan's name and slogan and worked it into our twentieth-anniversary marketing campaign. The unusual play on words was just what the product needed to make it go. I gave Wedgies away to all sorts of people. I even sent one to the governor, so I can say that I gave Arnold Schwarzenegger a wedgie. We came up with tiny packaging so we could sell them individually— we can give anyone a wedgie! And every month, we held a drawing and gave away a year's supply of Wedgies. We had a ball with the Wedgies idea. Every time I said "wedgie" I had to giggle.

Shakeups Can Be Good for You

After the sale of SBI, the online spinoff of my original company, Shari's Berries, I kept the right to use the Shari's Berries name in Sacramento, including my retail outlets. The new owners of SBI bought the Shari's Berries mark and received all sales outside of my retained area. I felt as though I'd lost a child. Because of the sale, I couldn't create products to be sold nationwide anymore!

I had to get back to my entrepreneurial roots and find a place to put my future ideas. I couldn't just let them fizzle out in the gloom.

The upside of this painful shakeup was that I was set free to develop a *new* business without territorial restrictions. After I was done mourning my first business, the word "new" came to life again. In 2006, the Berry Factory was born.

What a rebirth it was (and still is). Energy sizzled through me. New ideas cropped up so fast my legal pad got way too crowded with my scribbled notes. I planned to do things to strawberries that had never been done before. And why stop with strawberries? Why not grapes, bananas, cherries, raspberries, cookies, and wine?

This is where I am right now. Creativity never dies. It may go underground for a while, but it's only resting, gathering steam for its triumphant reemergence. I know this is true. I'll be dreaming up new strawberry creations and ways to package and sell them when I'm eighty—or maybe ninety-three, like Grannie.

A Berry Good Tip

Everyone has a creative side. Everyone has new, unique, and different ideas from time to time. But not everyone shares them. This is a shame.

My "berry good tip" is this: speak up! If you've got an idea, share it with someone. Don't keep it to yourself.

There are reasons why people don't speak up and share their new ideas. We might be afraid our idea will flop and we'll feel stupid. We fear that our idea will be so silly that people will laugh at us. We worry that we won't know how to develop the idea to its full potential. We fear that it will be too much work, or cost too much money, to make our idea happen. Or we're afraid someone else will steal our idea.

Yeah, okay. Maybe your idea is stupid and people will point at you and snicker, and your friends will pity you. Maybe you don't have enough money or knowhow to make it happen, and the whole thing blows up in your face or, worse, wilts at your feet. Maybe some unscrupulous nasty person takes your idea, runs with it, and makes a gazillion dollars. I guess all these scenarios are possible.

The thing is, they aren't very likely. It's much more possible that good things will happen when you share your ideas.

Try out your idea, either by telling someone about it or making a prototype. Maybe you will find out it's not such a great idea. Sometimes what sounded so good inside your head doesn't actually work in the real world. But you won't know that until you get that idea out there. If you test it and it doesn't work, you don't have to waste any more time and energy on it. You can move on to the next idea.

I have to laugh when people ask me if any of my ideas have flopped. Of course they have! On the other hand, so many of my ideas do work out. But by the time they get very far, they've been modified (sometimes again and again) to make the original idea even better or the process more efficient. That's because making the idea real allows me to see where the weaknesses are, so I can fix them. It also allows other people to give me feedback and suggestions on how to improve my idea. I always solicit other people's input. Sometimes your ideas may be in a larval stage—they're potential good ideas, but other people are needed to make them great. They'll say, "That's a good idea. But have you ever thought about trying it this way?" It happens all the time.

Finally, when you put your idea out there for others to see, you have validated it, made it concrete and real. If you hold your creativity inside, it can dry up. Let it out, and it will grow and multiply. Life goes by so fast. When you're old, do you want to reap a crop of bitterness because you never tried and now it's too late?

Speaking up about your ideas means you are serious. You have put a stake in the ground. It's a courageous act. So many of our ideas and dreams stay inside us simply because we are afraid. Take yourself, and your talents, seriously. We are here to share them, so that they may help others. Your creativity was given to you to use. So use it.

****

Shari's Secret Recipe #3
Mom's Strawberry Pie

Piecrust

18 graham crackers
¼ cup sugar
½ cup melted butter (not margarine!)

Strawberry Filling

1½ cups cold water
2 tbsp. cornstarch
1 3-oz. pkg. sugar-free strawberry gelatin
3 tbsp. sugar
4 cups hulled, sliced strawberries

For Piecrust: Crush graham crackers into a bowl. You should have approximately 1½ cups. Add sugar and melted butter and mix well.

Press the mixture firmly into a buttered 8-inch pie pan. Chill the crust in the refrigerator for about 45 minutes.

For Strawberry Filling: In a saucepan, mix together water and cornstarch. Bring this to a boil, stirring constantly. Turn down heat to medium and cook for about 2 minutes. Remove from heat and add the gelatin and sugar, mixing well until dissolved. Add the strawberries; mix together well.

Pour into graham-cracker crust. Place in refrigerator until set (about 2 hours). If desired, serve with whipped topping of your choice.

Chapter 4

Do It Right

Warm brown milk chocolate, slightly bitter yet slightly sweet dark chocolate, or silky smooth white chocolate—how do you choose between them?

Maybe it depends on your personality. Believe it or not, I can "read" what kind of a person you are based on what kind of dipped strawberry you order. So be careful what you choose in front of me.

Now, before you go thinking I'm a goofball, there is scientific proof that chocolate affects our moods. Chocolate increases the levels of endorphins, a feel-good chemical, in our bloodstream. Endorphins lessen pain and decrease stress. And chocolate contains a chemical called tryptophan, which causes the release of serotonin, which works as an anti-depressant. And there's more—phenyl ethylamine is also released by chocolate, which can lead to feelings of excitement that are similar to what we feel when we fall in love.

So don't tell me chocolate doesn't tell you something about personality.

When I started my business, I created a standard "beginners" set of six different berry designs to give people an idea of the flavors and designs available. I settled on a milk chocolate dip decorated with white swizzles (that's what we call the drizzled stripes across the berry); a milk chocolate dip with almonds; a white chocolate dip with dark swizzles; a white chocolate dip with coconut sprinkles; a dark chocolate dip with chocolate chip sprinkles; and the last, a berry dipped in half-white, half-dark.

Now dark chocolate is my favorite, and I love the chocolate chips sprinkled on top, making chocolate on chocolate, the darker the better. If you know chocolate like I do, you know that dark chocolate is the closest we get to the natural cocoa bean—it's the real thing. For some reason, more women than men prefer this berry version. And when a woman picks a dark with chocolate chips, it means first that

73

she really knows her chocolate and second that she is a very sensual, feminine woman!

White chocolate with coconut sprinkles is favored by a lot of men—big and strong guys with tons of masculine charm. (And yes, it is my husband Clay's favorite too.) Coconut is kind of a controversial topping. People either absolutely love it or absolutely hate it. If a manly guy walks into the store, you can bet he will be one who loves it. He'll want it on everything. But I only offer coconut sprinkled on milk or dark chocolate as a special order. That's because I think it looks like a horrible mess. But then, I'm not a big hardy guy.

And the people who like the half-white, half-dark berries? Those are the people who are pleasant, agreeable, and can get along with almost everybody. They're the best kind of customer to have. This berry's design was suggested by Clay, even though it didn't have any coconut. But I took all the credit for the design. After all, he's a contractor. What could he possibly know about berry designing?

I'm giving him credit now, though. I guess sexy guys who like coconut do know something about berries. But it's still my business to make sure those berries find the right home.

****

You may have noticed by now that my "secrets to success" are pretty simple. In fact, they are not secrets at all. I think anybody can be successful by doing a lot of hard work and putting out a quality product. Just make sure your product or service is the best it can be.

But simple does not mean easy.

What simple does mean is *focused*. When you start your business, don't try to specialize in everything. Offer one thing, or concentrate on one main thing, and make sure that one thing is the highest quality or the most unique. This is how you gain and keep your customers. After they know they can trust you to always deliver the best product in the best way at the best time, you can let them know about all the other great things you do. Right now my company offers hundreds of different variations, but I started with one. I was the "strawberry girl" doing chocolate-dipped strawberries—and that was it. It's still the foundation for everything we do.

But they aren't just any dipped strawberries. They are the *best*.

Quality Starts in the Dirt

The heart of any business is the product you offer. (If you have a service business, your service is your product.) But you don't make your product or run your business all by yourself. You probably get your ingredients or your tools from someone else. It's important that those "someones" be the best *they* can be.

I love my suppliers, especially my strawberry suppliers. I've used the same berry supplier for my entire berry career. They take great care of me, know me well and how picky I can be, and go to bat for me when I need them to.

I'm big on supporting your local businesses, which in my case means Sacramento, but I have to admit I cannot buy my strawberries from Sacramento growers. The fields and even the empty lots around Sacramento are filled with strawberries, but although they are a beautiful bright red and their smell alone makes you salivate, they're too full of sugar for our products. You have to eat them right away, and if you dip them into warm chocolate, they immediately fall apart and turn into strawberry mush.

Perfect berries for dipping are firm berries. Some companies selling dipped berries use unripe strawberries to make sure they are firm, but we don't. We buy strawberry varieties that are bred to be firm when perfectly ripe.

Perfect berries for dipping also must be big berries—we have written specs that we call "Shari's Pick." Large berries are necessary because we put so many goodies on top of the berry, such as coconut, nuts, or chocolate chips. Our berries must have muscle! I also like berries shaped like hearts, because I think they are more aesthetically pleasing. Sometimes we get a funkier longer shape from the wintertime Camarosa variety. They're red, big, and tasty, but they're shaped a little like a carrot. I use them, though, because the most important thing is taste.

We do add a lot of extras to our strawberries, but only to enhance their flavor, not overwhelm it. It has to feel good in your mouth. It should not be too crunchy, too soft, or even too chocolaty. And if it is too messy—if you can't eat it without dribbling it down your shirt—it is *really* not good.

We get most of our berries from Southern California in the wintertime and Central California in the summer. So even though they're not from Sacramento, at least we buy from California. California is the strawberry capital of the world—lucky me. But Mother Nature is not always kind, even to California (some growers say *especially* to California). If the weather is weird, it throws the strawberry clock off, and then we can be in a pickle. I have been forced to buy strawberries from New Zealand and fly them in at great expense just to make sure we get the best berries. I mean, it's not as if we can start making strawberries in the back room if we run out.

I guess you can tell I know my strawberries. I can trot out strawberry trivia at parties (this makes me very popular). Did you know that eight medium-sized strawberries have more vitamin C than an orange? Did you know there are about 23,000 acres of strawberries in California? California supplies 80 percent of the national strawberry inventory. If all the strawberries produced in California alone were laid berry to berry, they'd wrap around the world fifteen times. I bet you didn't know any of that. Well, you don't have to know. But I do, and so do my strawberry suppliers.

Then there's chocolate, my other basic ingredient. Not all chocolate is equal. For dipping, the chocolate needs to set firm and fast. It can't melt easily as it is being delivered. It needs to have that velvety-chocolate look, as if it will melt sweetly in your mouth.

And of course it needs to taste like heaven. I developed a buttery formula. It's waxy and glossy and perfect.

My dipping secrets need to remain my own—I can't give *all* my secrets away! But I'll let you in on one. If you want to dip your own strawberries at home, it's not that hard. At the end of this chapter is a dipping recipe you can follow. Maybe your berries won't be quite as fancy as mine, but you'll have fun making them, and so will your kids. You'll have fun eating them, too.

Do you know one of the reasons why my suppliers love working with me? I love working with them—and I let them know it. Even if someone drops the ball, we'll work it out, because we drop balls too sometimes. Together we catch most of them. We work together, and they feel proud that their berries or their chocolate are part of a product as good as ours.

Quality Timing

In my kind of business, we have to learn to expand and contract, and we have to do it fast. We are holiday driven. One Valentine's Day, we dipped over 400,000 berries and filled 35,000 orders—in three days! It was like planning for twenty huge fancy weddings all happening at the same time. Not only must everything be done at the right time, but everything must be *perfect*. My favorite day of the year is February 15.

Once there were three semi-trucks full of strawberries stuck in L.A. because of a snowstorm on the main highway, which stopped all traffic. It was the early morning of the day before Valentine's Day, and we—me and my temporary employees paid by the hour—were just sitting around waiting for the berries to arrive. Hours went by with no strawberries, and during this holiday an hour is a precious commodity. We fresh dip our strawberries within twenty-four hours of delivery, even on Valentine's Day. As we grew larger, this became harder, but this is a rule we never break. So I was a wreck by the time those strawberries finally arrived. I still don't know how we managed to dip, decorate, package, and ship our Valentine's Day orders on time. The good thing about this experience was that it shows that working with such a delicate, perishable product and doing it well keeps my competition to a minimum. It's darn hard!

Berries of Beauty

Why is it so important that we fresh dip our strawberries every day? Well, would you be impressed if you received a box of overripe strawberries oozing juice and covered with gooey melting chocolate? Probably not. Even if they tasted good, they wouldn't *look* good.

Looks are important. If your product is the best, it deserves to look like the best. Presentation is a big part of what I do—it's why I always loved wrapping gifts just as much as the gifts themselves. My products are more than just dipped berries—they are a complete experience. We pay meticulous attention to every single detail, trying to make each strawberry, each apple, and each bottle of wine a masterpiece. Each berry is hand-dipped, then drizzled with artistic color-coordinated designs. We place them individually in special fluted wrappers. Then we package them. Maybe they will come nestled in an elegant gold-foil, strawberry-red and chocolate-brown box or a specially designed rose-style gold box or . . . well, you get the idea.

There will be several layers of decorated cellophane protecting the creation and increasing the delicious suspense while you unwrap it. If the package has been shipped, it will arrive in a custom-designed white shipping container that is Styrofoam lined and ice-pack cooled, guaranteeing absolute freshness.

My retail stores also reflect my attention to aesthetic detail. When we opened our third retail outlet in 1998, we created a store that looked like an art gallery. It is elegant and a little off-the-wall. I wanted it to be a kind of Planet Hollywood. It has black and white floor tiles; an eight-foot-high, gold-framed, beveled-mirror menu; curved walls with inset, backlit window display boxes; faux finish on two walls; a granite-top counter; and a 5x3.5 theater-style light box spotlighting our long-stemmed strawberry roses. And when customers walk into the store, they find themselves looking at a strawberry-shaped wall adorned with a ten-foot-high photograph of a chocolate-dipped berry. Just walking into the shop makes you happy—and ready to buy something.

I aim to be like Tiffany. When you see their signature blue box with white satin ribbon around it, you know that the product inside is something extra-special. If Tiffany suddenly started wrapping its necklaces and rings in a different box, it would lose a lot of its magic. That's what the Berry Factory aims for. When you see one of my boxes, you know there is magic pixie dust all over what's inside.

People Are Even More Important than Berries

I ask a lot of my employees. But you know what—they always deliver! That's because I hire the best people I can find, provide lots of help and training, and treat them really, really well. It is impossible to run a quality business without quality people.

Because I run a holiday-driven business, we have to expand quickly, using a lot of brand-new people whom we hire just for the holidays. The winter holidays are big, Mother's Day is big, and the biggest of all is Valentine's Day. We usually do about one-sixth of our annual volume in the three days around Valentine's Day. On Valentine's Day at the Berry Factory, everyone comes to work. It doesn't matter who you are. Everyone from me on down is at work, doing whatever needs to be done: answering phones, dipping strawberries, sweeping the floor. I can usually even talk my vendor reps into helping—one

Valentine's Day my FedEx rep spent hours in our plant, packaging orders with us. (You can bet FedEx gets lots of our business!)

One of the reasons why I love my people so much is they put up with me. I can get a little crazy around the holidays, especially over quality. All our workers are individually trained in how to choose the right sized berry. Too-small berries are a big no-no. The instructions are very clear. One year I was sick with pneumonia on Valentine's Day. I came to work anyway, not to dip but to oversee the production and quality. When I got there, the first thing I saw was tray after tray with small dipped strawberries mixed in with the big ones. I was not pleased, but all I said was, "Pull out the small ones; put in big ones." The people who were done with their shifts came back and sorted the small ones out, while the new shift dipped and packaged the new trays with big berries. It was such a waste of chocolate, not to mention labor—both of which I was paying for.

Meanwhile I walked the line, checking on each person. And I kept finding those too-small berries being packaged! I tried to maintain my cool and patiently explain time after time why a berry was too small. I didn't feel good and I was rapidly becoming way too stressed. Finally, I had had it. I raised my voice and said, "Everybody's attention right here! I have an announcement!" Everyone stopped working to look at me. Then I took a too-small dipped strawberry out of a box and hurled it with all my strength against the wall. It made a splat and strawberry juice and chocolate oozed toward the floor. I said, *"No small berries!"*

That was the end of the small berries that day. In fact, one of my employees went around and took every small berry out of the room. Too bad I hadn't thought of that before.

Actually that was an unusual episode. Normally I don't get angry, and my employees usually don't make quality mistakes. When you are hired by the Berry Factory, the first place you go is training, which we affectionately call Berry Boot Camp.

Every new employee spends four hours at Berry Boot Camp, working a variety of jobs while paired with a seasoned employee. No matter what job you're applying for—delivery driver, counter salesperson in the store, working on the phones, dipping and decorating—you get to find out what that job is like. Not only can we find out if the new employee has what it takes to be successful with us, the employee can find out if they like working here. Our aim is to put each person in the position that is right for them. I want everyone who works for me to enjoy their work and have fun. When you enjoy your work, you're much more likely to do it well. If someone loves working with numbers or computers, they're probably not going to be happy dipping strawberries. But there are others who love to play with food and make it look beautiful—they're going to make good dippers or decorators. In Berry Boot Camp, they get to make a tuxedo berry and a berry blossom bouquet, and they get to wrap a basket all by themselves. We watch them to see if they are smiling. If they are, we know that we have a good one.

I know that my company is only as strong as its weakest employee. I treat them all with TLC. Even my temporary and contract employees feel as if they are a part of something wonderful, something that makes people happy. I once read that your employees will only take as good care of your customers as you take care of them. I have proven this to be true. My employees not only love their jobs, they love their customers.

It All Comes Down to Customers

That's what it's all about, isn't it? Your product or service is not really about you. It's about how well you can serve others—your customers. Without them, you might as well go home.

I learned when I was working at a department store during college that the customer is always right. It's such a simple philosophy, but it goes a long way with your customers. Don't you hate it when somebody argues with you when you're buying something from them? This is my pet peeve. Nobody ever argues with a customer at the Berry Factory, because she is always right. We will do whatever it takes to make her happy.

We market mostly to women aged twenty-five to fifty-four. We have many men ordering from us, too, but I know that's because women are taping our brochures to bathroom mirrors where their men will see them. Our products have become a tradition in many households on Valentine's Day or Mother's Day. Many guys will tell us they have to order from us because "she" expects them to. One man even told me that when he forgot to order from us on Valentine's Day, his wife was so upset she threatened divorce!

When people give gifts, they want to make a big impression, and that's why our high-quality products are so popular. People will buy the best for someone else, even if they won't for themselves. They will spend more money on someone they love than they will on themselves. When someone is searching for a special gift, they rarely look for something cheap.

The heart of our business *is* heart. We truly care about our customers, because they make us part of the important events in their lives. We are there for engagements, weddings, birthdays, graduations, baby showers, and retirement parties. When people want to show their love for each other, they give our products. Now how wonderful is that? Who could work here and not feel good?

One time a couple got engaged right in the middle of our store. The guy had worked it out with us beforehand—he put the ring box in with the berries. She had no idea he was going to propose; she thought they just came in for a special snack. About five of us were watching secretly through the one-way glass in my office. She found the ring and threw her arms around his neck. Then he slipped the ring on her finger, they ate the berries (she had to eat hers through tears), and they left holding hands.

Another time, a man came in with an $11,000 engagement ring and bought one of our little gold boxes with six strawberry roses inside. We helped him hide the ring inside the box. He said he'd let us know how it went. He didn't have to, because the next week his fiancée came in flashing the ring and asked if we recognized it. When I asked her if she was surprised, she said she was so excited about the strawberries she didn't even notice the ring!

Then there was the man who wanted us to take a huge diamond ring—it must have been at least two karats—smoosh it into a strawberry, and dip the whole thing in chocolate. I talked him out of it, though. I was afraid his girlfriend might break a tooth.

Of course, there's the other side of love, too. One Valentine's Day I was working the phones, which were ringing off the hook. I got a call from a guy who was sent an anonymous Valentine's Day gift. "You have to tell me who this is from," he demanded. Now, I was the person who actually took the order, so I knew who it was from; but the persistent woman who ordered it insisted that it remain anonymous, and she was our customer. So I said I couldn't tell him.

"You don't understand," he protested. "I *have* to know who these are from! If they are from my wife, and I go home and don't thank her for them, I'm in trouble. But if they *aren't* from my wife, and I go home and thank her for them, then I'm in trouble."

I said, "You're in trouble."

I guess he was a wealthy guy, because he offered me a year of memberships to a health club, then a country club, if I would just tell him. But I kept replying, "I'm sorry, sir," while trying not to laugh. Finally I said, "I have to go now." I sometimes wonder what he did.

The stories can be sad. Every year we'll have at least one woman who orders a box of strawberry roses to go to herself at her office, so the people she works with will think she has a Valentine.

Whatever their stories, our customers make us part of their lives. I am grateful to my customers, and I want them to have the best.

That Long Extra Mile

Here's another cliché that I built my business on: go the extra mile. (I told you my secrets weren't really secrets!) Whatever you have to do to make your customers happy, do it.

This is another simple thing that isn't easy. In the early years of my business, I offered catering services for my local customers. I'd prepare meat and cheese trays, fruit trays, or breakfast trays, as well as my signature dipped berries. I found a great deli nearby where I bought my cheese and meats. One week I was catering a meeting to be held on a Sunday, and my deli guy suggested that I pick up the meat and cheese on Sunday morning, even though he was normally closed that day. That way it will be nice and fresh, he said. "What a great guy," I thought—until that Sunday, when I arrived at his store. He had forgotten all about it and the store was closed. And my meeting was soon!

I could have just brought fruit, muffins, and strawberries to the meeting. I had those, and my customers probably wouldn't be upset. In fact, they might not even notice what was missing. But that's not what I promised. So I called Clay and asked him to run to the nearest grocery store and buy an assortment of deli meat and cheese that I could place on a tray. But when Clay got to the store, he found they had a power outage and couldn't slice anything! So I had him buy a chunk of meat and bring it to me, as I had a meat slicer. I sliced all the meats and cheese myself so fast it's a wonder I still have ten fingers! But I got it all done and walked in the door exactly two minutes before the meeting began.

I have done every job within my company, and I still do them when necessary. I want all my employees to feel the same way. Whatever it takes, whatever the customer wants, whenever the customer wants it, we make it happen. If they want it delivered Sunday night and I can make arrangements, it will get done, no problem. If they want coconut sprinkles on top of Jelly Bellies, okay. If they want green ribbon on a pink package, we'll do it and not mention once that green and pink look terrible together.

Honesty Really Is the Best Policy

Yeah, it's another cliché. I'm full of them. The hardest thing to be honest about is when you have made a mistake. I hate to make mistakes, and I'm just like everyone else—I hate to admit to them. But I have learned that the best way to handle my mistakes is to be honest and say, "I made a mistake. And this is what I'm going to do about it." Then I do whatever it is I said I would do.

I used to agonize over mistakes and drive myself and everyone around me crazy. I remember a really bad Valentine's Day, in my sixth year of business. The delivery company we used made errors on *100* of our orders. At that time, that was a big percentage of the day's total. I was devastated. I felt violated. Now, I admit that at that time I was four months pregnant with Hogan, so maybe hormones contributed to my state of mind, but the nausea I felt had just as much to do with my business. I had worked so hard to have a clean reputation. I worked hard to be sure that nobody heard anything bad about me, only good. And now I had 100 angry customers. I felt that my reputation was ruined for all time.

After working this thirty-six-hour shift, I drove to my friends George and Joy's house. I had met them at church, and they had become like substitute parents to me: warm, loving, wise Christian people. When I walked in their door, I was in tears, and my head was hanging down. George took one look at me and gave me a big hug. I told him what had happened, and I'll never forget what he said. It was so simple.

He said, "Shari, don't get so upset. As long as you handle it correctly and learn something from it, it is a blessing."

Blubbering as I was, I didn't hear him at first. He was way too calm, and I thought, "What is he talking about? Blessing? I don't think so." How could these terrible mistakes be a blessing? I wasn't kidding about terrible—some of the deliveries were a day late, others never showed up at all, more than a few had been delivered dumped upside down, and still others had sunflower-seed shells in the packages!

But George was right. Those mistakes were opportunities to show my customers what kind of a company I really ran. It all depended on what I did next.

The first thing we did was redeliver all hundred of those orders the very next day—fresh and complete and right this time. I brought in delivery people from anywhere I could find them.

Next, I didn't charge the customers for the original messed-up order or the replacement. I gave everyone their money back.

Finally, I sent each of them a signed personal letter apologizing for the mistake and included a gift certificate for the amount they had originally spent, which they could use in the future if they would ever trust me again.

While we were making these amends, one of the customers whose order never showed up paid us a personal visit the next morning at one of our brand-new retail stores. It was on the ground floor of a high-rise office building, and the customer was a lawyer who worked in the same building. He raised a big stink while we were all scrambling to get the replacement orders out. He basically ripped my employee in half in front of everybody. It was ugly. He steamed back upstairs, leaving all of us shaken.

We resent his order anyway and gave him his money back, and I sent him my personal letter with the gift certificate that very day.

Now here's the great part. At least *eight* years later, my husband, Clay, who is a swimming pool contractor, was hired to build a pool for this same lawyer. It is Clay's standard practice, at the completion of a job, to bring his customer a box of berries as a thank-you for the business. So when the pool was completed (it was beautiful), Clay showed up with a box of berries in hand and told the guy that he was "Mr. Berry."

"You're kidding me!" said the lawyer. When Clay answered no, he really was married to the Strawberry Lady, his customer responded, "I've got to tell you a story. I ordered a gift box of berries a long time ago, and the delivery was messed up. I was livid because my wife didn't get her Valentine's Day gift. I'm a lawyer in your wife's building, so I went down to her store and yelled and screamed and swore I'd never buy from her again—and threatened to tell everyone I knew what a crappy company she owned.

"But you know what?" he continued. "I was so impressed by the way she handled that mistake—she took full responsibility, and then she made it right—and more so. I've been her customer ever since and have referred her to everyone I know."

The Real Shari

One of the philosophies of my business is that people do business with people. Customers want to know there's a real person behind a catalog or Web site. A "real Shari" behind my brand is another form of quality assurance.

I've always known this. After personally writing the Grand Opening mailer for my first retail outlet in 1991, I continued to handwrite every holiday and postcard mailer, even as my customer list grew larger and larger. I know that this personal touch helped me build my brand. Even today, when my mailing list is over 30,000 customer names strong, I am proud that not one of those names is from a purchased list. They are all real customers who buy my products (although of course I no longer personally handwrite 30,000 holiday mailers—if I did, that'd be *all* I did!).

I'm also personally involved in marketing and promotion. I love this aspect of my business, so I'm a "hands-on" marketer. I write my own press releases. I write, star in, and produce my own radio commercials and video ads. I often do the design for my ads, Web site, and marketing literature. And of course I'm always thinking of new ways to promote the Berry Factory.

After my original company was purchased and I was no longer involved in Shari's Berries nationwide, I was reminded again and again how important it was for my customers to feel that they were dealing with a "real Shari."

I believe that the company that bought the Shari's Berries Web site didn't feel this way. To me it seemed as if they felt it would be more efficient and profitable to be "all business"; that customers cared more about saving money than they did about doing business with people they liked and trusted.

If that's what they believed, then I'm pretty sure they're wrong. After a magazine article came out about the Web site division of my company being sold, I was swamped by customer calls demanding, "Is this the real Shari? I only want to buy from that woman's company." When I exhibited at state fairs and trade shows, people wanted proof I was the real Shari before they'd buy a box of berries. I remember at one state fair, a big, tough, black-leather-wearing biker dude with a long full beard came up to me. "You the real Shari?" he asked. I said I was. "Are you sure?" he persisted. It took me a while to convince him I was the real Shari before he'd buy anything.

And it's not just the customers who care about the personal touch. It's the vendors and advertisers too. One of my challenges when I started the Berry Factory was how to approach the national contacts I'd made during my years as the founder of Shari's Berries without being tacky or negative about my former company. But it turned out to be so easy. As soon as they understood that my new company was the Berry Factory, my relationships with these key contacts were right back where they had been. People do business with individuals they like and trust. This principle holds true for everyone.

When You Do It Right, People Notice

There is a saying: "When somebody's happy with your product or service, they tell three people. When they're unhappy, they tell twelve."

Quality sells itself. When you put out a quality product or service that you guarantee 100 percent, and back it up with superior customer service, your chances of success are great.

You might even win awards. My company was voted the best product made in Sacramento—more than once. We won over Intel and Campbell's soup! We won a "Best Gift Basket" award seven years in a row. I personally have won numerous business awards. And I even won an award for "Best Martini in Sacramento." (In chapter 8 I'll give you my recipe!)

Another benefit from quality is that you can charge more. People expect to pay more for excellence. There are other companies that chocolate-dip strawberries, and many of them are cheaper than ours.

They might sell for $1.25, while ours sell for $3.00. But you know, it's like comparing Walmart to Nordstrom. We might sell the same item, but ours is a patented, trademarked, unique product that we deliver year round and nationwide. We do not sell berries unless they have been dipped the same day they're sent out for delivery. We buy from the best strawberry growers there are, on a weekly basis to get the best that Mother Nature offers, while our competitors may have annual contracts forcing them to buy whatever is available from that grower no matter how it looks or tastes.

I never wanted to sell a cheap product, just so I could have a higher volume. After I lost control of my company and the new CEO started eliminating "useless" things such as beautiful packaging in order to save pennies a box, it tore me up inside. My artistic creation was reduced to a commodity that had nothing special about it.

At the Berry Factory, we know that no one wants to give a cheap, unimpressive gift. Gifts are a reflection of your feelings for the recipient. When someone sends you a gift from the Berry Factory, you know that someone likes you a lot.

I like being high priced. My customers get what they pay for. They're not just paying for a chocolate-dipped strawberry. They're paying for the quality, the service, and the magic.

However, in a difficult economy, I also know that it's important to offer lower-priced options. So at the Berry Factory we have come up with simpler packaging that allows our customers to still have excellent berries at a reduced price. But we don't compromise on the quality of the product. And we will always keep our top-shelf options. If you want the very best, it will be available.

The biggest reason to "do it right" is pride in yourself and your product. If I cut some corners, I might have more customers, but I doubt they would be happier customers. I would rather take the higher road, even if I sell less. I am secure knowing that I always do the best that I can. One of my favorite lines from Scripture is, "No good thing will the Lord withhold from those who do what is right" (Psalms 84:11b).

A Berry Good Tip

I think that a dedication to the best quality must be a part of everything you do. You can't depend on excellent product alone to get you where you want to go. You need excellent customer service too. Even if you have the lowest price or the fastest delivery, you will not have a quality reputation if your customers don't know that you care about them. And you always have to try to do right in your personal life too, because if your business isn't personal, you're in trouble. You need it all in order to be successful.

There is a T-shirt vendor in Sacramento whom I used to use for promotional T-shirts. What a great artist he is! His designs are always creative and colorful—they get you noticed every time. He uses only the highest-quality T-shirts. His prices are reasonable. He's a super nice guy, easygoing and funny.

And he's always—always—late with delivery. Sometimes he's very late. His accounting and administrative work is sloppy, and he makes lots of promises that he can't seem to keep. He seldom returns calls or answers e-mails.

Every time I complained, he was apologetic and said he'd do better next time. Only this didn't happen. Each next time was just the same—wonderful product that came late. So you guessed it. Eventually I reluctantly had to stop buying from him and find a new T-shirt vendor.

It makes me so frustrated! I love his product, but I can't rely on him. As a friend and fan of his work, I told him, "Get yourself a secretary, or someone who can do the day-to-day stuff while you're off being an artist." So far he hasn't taken my advice.

That's the price he is paying for not offering quality in every aspect of his business. But here's an extra tip: I still keep this guy on my list of potential vendors. I don't burn bridges, ever. You never know when you're going to need someone. Maybe someday my favorite T-shirt artist will wise up and hire someone to help him, and I can do business with him again.

* * * *

Shari's Secret Recipe #4
Melted Dipping Chocolate

1 12-oz. bag semisweet chocolate chips (or white chocolate chips or butterscotch chips)

¼ tsp. orange, hazelnut, or mint extract or liqueur (optional)

Put chips in microwave-safe bowl. Microwave on *defrost* setting (very important) for 3 to 4 minutes. Stir. Return to microwave for another 2 to 3 minutes. Stir. Repeat until chips are completely melted. If desired, add liqueur or flavored extract.

Pour melted chocolate into fondue pot or Crockpot. Keep warm on lowest setting and place on a table for dipping goodies (see the next chapter!). Stir occasionally if necessary.

Chapter 5

Clap Until Your Hands Hurt

If you had twenty teenagers at your house for a party, what would you serve them? Potato chips and sour-cream dip? Tortilla chips and salsa? Pretzels and soda? Hamburgers and pizza? Cake and cookies?

Bo-ring! Mix it up a little. If you have to serve pizza, make it chocolate-strawberry pizza. If you have to serve chips and salsa, try strawberry salsa.

But if you want to be really popular—and what teenager doesn't want to be popular?—you'll serve them what I do at the parties I give for my sons, or for anyone, for that matter. I serve the same thing for a little kids' party or a fancy, high-heels, grownup soiree. Whatever your age, if I invited you to one of my parties, what you'd remember for years afterward would be the do-it-yourself dessert buffet.

So let's pretend: welcome to my party. Get in line and help yourself.

But first, the rules. They are pretty simple. 1: No double-dipping. 2: No finger-licking until after you're done collecting ingredients. 3: Let your inner artist come out to play.

Start at table #1, a small card table covered with a white tablecloth. White linen would be beautiful, but it's a lot more practical to use plastic, even at an adult party. Adults can get messy too. Or the table will be covered with a Disney cartoon tablecloth if you're a little kid or a bright red or blue paper tablecloth if you're a teenager. Pick up a paper plate of a coordinating color to the tablecloth. Next you'll see a big stack of ten-inch squares of wax paper. Lay one of these on top of your paper plate.

Move on to table #2. This is a long table filled end to end with goodies that you will spear with toothpicks, layering them on each toothpick until just the decorative ribbon at the tip is showing. These goodies will include individual green or red seedless grapes, pineapple chunks, mandarin orange segments, and maraschino cherries. You'll also find licorice pieces, miniature marshmallows, and big fat ones too. And a variety of cookies—my boys like Oreos the best, but Nutter Butter and fortune cookies are always popular too. For people who love the salty stuff, there are pretzel sticks and pretzel rounds. You can place the cookies and pretzels next to your speared items. Finally, of course (you knew this was coming), there are ripe, red strawberries. There are always strawberries. (I can get the very best!) Mix and match to suit your own tastes. By the time you reach the end of this table, your plate will hold skewers laden with edible art in the process of becoming.

Finally, move on to the last table. You know what you'll find, of course—chocolate—rich, melted, gooey chocolate keeping warm in a fondue or Crockpot. Depending on how ambitious I feel, you might even find another Crockpot full of melted butterscotch or white vanilla coating. Dip in your toothpick creations and your cookies and pretzels and swirl them around until they are evenly covered.

Before the chocolate sets, decorate your art. There are small bowls full of coconut, chopped almonds, chocolate chips, confetti-colored sprinkles, crushed peppermint candy, mini M&Ms, small Jelly Belly candies, and other surprises. Be wild if you like—mix nuts and coconut together, or peppermint and sprinkles, or pile on every topping you can fit. Or be elegantly simple and position a single piece of almond on top of one chocolate-covered grape. Anything goes!

Place your edible art carefully on the wax paper square, where the chocolate will harden into a perfect gloss. Before you pick it up and put it in your mouth, let your eyes feast on its beauty.

* * * *

I told you how I love to give gifts. Gifts are a visible way of saying, "I value you." Gifts aren't always things. Words and actions show your appreciation too.

If you want to be successful at business or life, one of the most important things you can do is spread a lot of compliments around. People love to be appreciated. This is true of me, you, your family, friends, customers, employees, and suppliers. Even your enemies like to be appreciated. It's a universal human condition.

Appreciation is what I'm all about, in my personal life and business life. It's one of the things I do best and a primary key to my success.

Maybe that's why Valentine's Day plays such a big part in my life. That's the day you show those you love how much you appreciate them. Customers flock to my door (or my Web site) from February 12 through February 14. During those three days, the Berry Factory earns about one-sixth of our annual revenue—in three days! That's what appreciation can do for you. If your product or service gives people a way to show it, you've got it made.

Following the rule of "always show your appreciation" has brought me success in all areas of my life, not just business. That's what romance is at its heart, right?

Treat Me Good: It's Charming

Here's another success tip: pick a great mate. I know "lucky in love" is a cliché, but oh, it's so true in my case. I'm so grateful for my husband. Clay is a huge factor in my success. I knew he was the right one for me when I was sixteen, although it wasn't the right time. I needed to mature, and now I'm glad I got that time, because it ensured that when Clay and I did come together again, I appreciated him even more.

It took Clay a little longer than me to come to the same realization. But I grew on him, I think he kind of got used to being treated so good, although today he teases me that I "stalked" him.

I'm not exaggerating when I say that I still get butterflies when we kiss, even after all these years. When I hear his sexy voice on the phone, my muscles turn to jelly. He has a way of saying goodbye, almost in a deep whisper—it's like a promise of good things to come. I guess you could say we have chemistry.

He's not a conventionally romantic guy. He does bring me flowers and sentimental cards he writes himself, but they don't always show up when I think they're going to. The flowers have become less frequent the longer we've been married, but I don't mind because the love notes he writes in the cards he sends me are so beautiful. But the love poems he has written me are under lock and key and I've been sworn to secrecy—I had to promise that they are for my eyes only and I will take them to my grave.

He trained our boys to hand-make cards for me, and this collection is more precious than any of my other treasures. Sometimes they are pretty funny. One Valentine's Day, Max made a card for Clay's mom, Donna, that said, "Even though you are old and wrinkled, you have the heart of a teenager." Luckily Donna is great and she loved it. She said, "It's so true!"

Clay's gifts are always unexpected and unusual. He's like Ben that way. I loved it in Ben, and I love it in Clay. Take his marriage proposal, for instance. Although we'd been living together for nearly four years, and I'd been in love with him for ten, I had no idea if he was ever going to propose. I didn't talk to Clay about marriage because I was going to be smart the second time around with him. I lost him the first time, and I thought I would die. I wasn't going to make the mistake of pushing him. I knew marriage had to be his idea.

The only time I'd ever mentioned marriage was when we first moved in together. I told him if I was going to wear a piece of jewelry for the rest of my life—like an engagement ring—I wanted to pick it out. He agreed, and that was that. There was no more mention of marriage, for four long years. Clay is a guy who takes his time. He wants to be certain he's doing the right thing.

Certainty struck him on Labor Day weekend, 1991. We were in Oregon on a camping trip with his family. On Sunday morning, Clay's mom, Donna, made a fantastic four-course breakfast for all of us, working on her tiny trailer stove. I don't know how she does it. Everybody ate too much. My stomach felt as if I'd swallowed a balloon.

"Get your things, Shari," Clay said. "We're going for a boat ride."

Now, I felt so overstuffed that all I wanted to do was lie around on a lounge chair. But Clay's voice sounded suspicious, like he was up to something. As we were getting into the car, his stepdad put his arm around Clay's shoulder and I overheard him say, "Your mom would really like to see you do this. I think Shari's ready."

We got into the car and drove to the campground lodge, where the boat rental was. As we got out of the car, Clay asked, "Uh, why don't you go in the store and buy some snacks for the boat while I take care of the rental?"

Snacks! We had both just eaten enough breakfast to feed six hungry loggers. It was obvious he was trying to get rid of me. He kept digging around in his golf bag in the back of the car. Suddenly I felt more energetic. Something was going on—it occurred to me that he wanted to look for wherever he'd put the ring.

I tried to play it cool, but my heart was pounding. I wandered into the lodge and suddenly felt that I was going to puke. I made it to the bathroom and sat there, thinking, "Oh my gosh, he's going to propose," over and over. Nausea and elation fought for my stomach. "What if I'm wrong," I argued with the Shari who wanted to throw up, trying to calm myself down. "It's probably just my imagination or wishful thinking. I shouldn't get too excited, because if he doesn't propose I'll be so upset." But I knew deep in my heart I wasn't wrong.

I finally made it out of the bathroom and down to the boat dock. Clay told me they were out of boats, so he had rented a canoe. If you've never been in a canoe, let me tell you they are wobbly, especially when the wind's up, which it was. A canoe proposal didn't sound very likely, or romantic either, but the tense yet hopeful look on Clay's face said differently.

We got into the canoe without falling in the lake—a good start. We were paddling with the wind, so we made it to the middle of the lake quickly. "Let's stop and sit here for a minute," Clay said. Then, while my hair blew over my face and into my eyes, he gave me his spiel—how much he loved me and would I be his forever, and more like that, only I can't remember exactly what he said, and neither can he. We were both in shock about what was happening at last. The only words I really remember were: "marry me?"

The wind picked up even more, making the canoe shake as he handed me a ring box. My hands shook too, because I didn't know how I was going to react. Would I be able to pretend I liked the ring I told him not to pick out without me? I was afraid I'd blow it. I don't have a very good poker face.

But I didn't need to worry about ruining anything. He had remembered—he bought a marquise solitaire diamond ring (my favorite shape) on a simple gold band, so I could finish the design myself, just like I wanted.

I wanted so much to hug and kiss him at that moment, but I couldn't. He was too far away from me to get my arms around him. I was afraid the canoe would tip over, the wind was blowing so hard. I put that beautiful diamond on my finger, picked up the paddle, and suddenly realized how very far away we were from the boat dock. We paddled hard against the wind back to the dock, and it wasn't until we got on land that I got to throw my arms around him.

Back at the campsite, everyone was sitting around waiting for us to come back from our boat ride. Clay broke out the bottle of Dom

Perignon he had hidden in the car, and he announced to everyone that he had just proposed and I'd accepted. There were cheers, tears, kisses, and hugs. Clay's mom, Donna, got out a calendar and started going over dates, which made Clay look a little green. The shock was starting to wear off and he realized his life had just changed.

Uppermost in my mind was that I had to tell Grannie. I had promised her that she would be the first person I told if and when I got engaged. So I roused Clay from his stupor and we jumped on our bikes and rode down to the market to call Grannie and tell her.

And that's when I felt married already. The wedding was just a formality.

Pay Attention

I guess you can tell that I appreciate my husband, and I let him know it. And it's not one-sided. Clay knows how to show that he appreciates me. He knows that I love to give gifts—you can bet that he loves me giving *him* gifts! Clay found a way to make it even more enjoyable for me.

Wherever I've lived, I always had a special place to keep my gift-giving supplies. When I was a little girl, it was under my bed. As a single girl in my one-bedroom apartment, it was a corner of the living room. Wherever it was, it was always the messiest place in the house, cluttered with wrapping paper, ribbons, glue sticks, scissors, tape, sequins, fabric roses, gift cards, gift boxes, and even a stash of extra gifts so I'm never caught short on something to give.

You never know when a gift will make someone's day, especially when it's not their birthday. It doesn't matter how inexpensive the gift is—a box of strawberries doesn't cost much in the universal scheme of things. The important things are that you know what the person likes and the gift is beautifully presented. Whether it's an appetizer taken to a potluck, a hostess gift, or making a dessert for your kids, those extra touches make a huge increase in the gift's perceived value.

When we were first married, Clay built me a replica of an antique pie safe to keep my gift supplies in. A pie safe is a cupboard with mesh screens instead of doors, and it was where frontier ladies used to keep their freshly baked pies, allowing the pies to breathe yet keeping them safe from animals and birds—or hungry children.

I love my pie safe, not only because it's a way to keep my hobby of giving fancy wrapped gifts from taking over the house, but because Clay made it for me. He pays attention to my likes and dislikes. Paying attention is the best and most personal way to show your appreciation for someone. It makes them feel that you really see them, and you like what you see.

Seek and You Shall Find

Sometimes it's not that easy to discover what makes some people happy. Some people have built up defense systems designed to keep people away, so they won't get hurt. But I think these people may have the most to teach us about the value of appreciation.

So far I haven't said much about my father, in whose garden I learned to love strawberries. My parents split up when I was only seven, and I lived with my mom and Ben. The divorce was hard on my dad. It wasn't something he wanted. Of course, when I was a child I had no idea what losing his wife and daughters meant to him. All I knew was that I resented having to go to his house every other weekend, when I would rather have been at home with my mom. My relationship with my dad was difficult for a long time.

Like many people in Klamath Falls, my dad worked in the lumber industry. He was a mill laborer for almost forty years, a job he tolerated because it paid fairly well with good benefits. He was able to take early retirement when only in his late fifties, but retirement didn't change him much. He was, and is, a man set in his ways; he lives alone and follows the same routine he's had for decades. He has little patience for anything new or different from what he's always done. Today I often refer to him as a true hillbilly.

But I say it with real affection. I've learned to appreciate him. I gave up wishing he was different, and I pay attention to who he is. I look for the good stuff in him, and guess what? The good stuff is there.

I show my appreciation in my favorite way, of course—I give him gifts! My sister, Dayna, complains that our dad is impossible to buy for, but that's because she hasn't figured him out yet. She gets him things that she thinks he should like. But he rarely does.

For one thing, he doesn't like "things" so much; he's proud of living simply. He's tight with money—a trait that I share. He also doesn't like to be told what he should like. He doesn't want to be pushed out of his comfort zone. He will only like something if he thinks it's his own idea. I have learned to set him up for an opportunity and let him take the bite. If he does, great—it's his own idea. If he doesn't, that's okay too. It just means I have more information about him.

For instance, I found out he likes old Western movies, especially those starring John Wayne. I also know he doesn't like computers or anything remotely technical. But when I told him I could get old Western movies online for about five dollars, he was excited. John Wayne for almost nothing—now that he liked! So I bought him an inexpensive DVD player, and every Father's Day and Christmas I get him another classic Western for his collection. I wrap it up in fancy wrapping paper and we already know he's going to like what's inside when he opens it up. It takes him forever to open up the packages because he wants to reuse the paper.

His delight makes me happy too. Yet here's my sister spending all this money, and all she gets is aggravation because he didn't like the thing she thought would be so perfect. She's still hoping he'll change, I guess.

One of the best gifts I gave my Dad wasn't something I could wrap up. My dad comes to visit us in Sacramento twice a year. One day on his visit a few years ago, he was watching TV, because we have more channels than he does and he likes to watch old sitcoms. His favorite is the 1960s series "The Beverly Hillbillies." He's a big fan of Max Baer, Jr., who played Jethro Bodine. (That right there tells you a lot about my dad.)

"Before I die," Dad said after the show, "I'd do just about anything to meet ol' Jethro."

I remembered a newspaper article I'd read about Max Baer possibly opening a casino in Carson City. The article mentioned that he lived in South Lake Tahoe, which is only about an hour's drive from where I live. I thought, "I bet Max Baer has a Web site," and sure enough, he does. I sent an e-mail explaining who I was and how my dad was a fan, with Dad leaning over my shoulder as I typed.

Fifteen minutes later, I got a reply from Max Baer's assistant—who just happened to be a big fan of my berries! Together we worked on setting up a dinner, and six months later during my dad's next visit, we made the trip up to Tahoe and had a three-hour dinner with "Jethro Bodine"! Max and my dad got along great, although my dad was nearly speechless and stared at Max for the entire time. After dinner, Max gave us a big bag of signed memorabilia and personally drove us back to our hotel. As Max drove away, my stunned father said, "Wow, I got to ride in the back of Jethro's rig—it just doesn't get any better than that." Since then we've met several times with Max on Dad's semiannual trips, although Dad is no longer speechless. He loves to argue—loudly—with Max.

Paying attention to my dad's likes and dislikes has made me realize that I'm like him in many ways, and not only that we're both tighter than a drum! I got my love of sweets from him. What a sweet tooth that man has! He likes to play video poker, just like Grannie and me. (He loved Grannie, and I think losing her in the divorce was as big a blow as losing his daughters.) But most of all, we're both sentimental fools.

His sentimental streak came as a surprise to me. I had always seen him as so crusty and stubborn, so "my way or the highway." But for years after Dayna and I had grown up and married, he kept our childhood toys in "our" room in his house. He just couldn't bring himself to get rid of them. When he drives to Reno to play video poker, he still stops at the same rest stop he and my mom stopped at when they once vacationed in Reno, so he can sit on the rock my mom sat on that day, when they were still in love.

Every Valentine's Day I get a big fancy Valentine from my dad. It's usually a card with a big red heart and a sentimental message handwritten by him in two colors of ink. He sticks a $100 bill in there too; he doesn't shop so that's what he's always done. I love that he uses two kinds of ink on my Valentine's card. Presentation is important to him too. He wants that card to be special because it's a reflection of how he feels about me.

Because I made an effort to know my dad as he really is, I got a reward: I found out he's a good man who loves me. But the biggest reward was finding out how much I love him.

Turning Customers into Family

When I opened my first retail store in 1991, I had 3,000 customers. I know exactly how many there were because I personally wrote—by hand—the Grand Opening mailers we sent to each and every one of them. I continued doing this for years for every holiday and postcard mailer. I think this personal touch helped me to build my brand. I also showed up in person at various events around town with berries I gave away.

For a couple of years I made most of my deliveries myself, which meant I spent a lot of time on the road. This was a challenge, because I wanted to be accessible to my customers any time they wanted me, and this was before cell phones. So I had my calls transferred to a pager and I made it a rule to always return my calls within ten minutes. I worked hard to get that phone to ring, and I didn't want my customers and suppliers to have any doubts about how much I valued their calls. When my pager went off, I immediately began looking for a pay phone—I kept a bucket of quarters in my car. It wasn't long before I knew the location of every pay phone in Sacramento!

When my customer list got larger, I sent out presents every year to my top 100 customers, with another handwritten note from me, telling them how much I appreciated their business. When cell phones became available, you can bet I got one, and again if I missed a call I returned it as soon as possible.

In short, I treated my customers as if they were my family. Guess what—they started treating me the same way! Appreciation begets appreciation.

The Best Place to Work

I've never had to work too hard to convince people to work for me. You get to eat your mistakes, for one thing. You can always tell who the new girl is because she has smears of chocolate near the corners of her mouth. During the holidays, we employ hundreds of temp workers and they usually agree it's one of their best temp gigs.

The only employee I've ever had to beg to come to work with me was my very first one. ReNida was the Mary Kay representative in my first networking group. I loved the way she went at things. But at first she was reluctant to come to work for a startup berry dipper—gee, I can't understand why, can you? Finally she agreed to come for just a few months, since she was due to start an accounting class. Twenty years later, she still works for me. She's done nearly every job in the company, just as I have.

As the company grew, I have been a dipper, delivery girl, secretary, accountant, saleslady, janitor, packer, and shipper. I know how hard my employees work, because I used to do their job. (And sometimes I still do, when it's holiday crunch time.) This is at the core of why I respect them so much and treat them so well. I appreciate my employees, and they know it.

This is another key to my success—I always take great care of my employees. Remember: your employees will never treat your customers any better than you treat them. I would never expect an employee to do anything I wouldn't do myself. We're a team. I know that's another cliché, but so what? It's a cliché that works.

My company has won "Best Place to Work" awards because of one thing: my staff feels appreciated for the work they do. They feel that the company belongs to them. It's much more than the competitive benefits package and the product discounts they receive. I try to be creative in showing how much I value my employees. At various times over the years, I've rewarded employees with cash bonuses on their hiring anniversaries or gifts of jewelry or event tickets on their birthdays. I've given out manicures, pedicures, and massages for Easter and Christmas, trips to Disneyland, and cruises to Mexico. They have been allowed to send berry arrangements once a month to a recipient of their choice. I encourage employees to share their ideas, and I always listen. I want my employees to feel as if this is their company.

Of course, I give gifts and parties—I wouldn't be *me* if I didn't, right? The best gifts are the most personal, like the time I gave my warehouse manager a pair of boxer shorts printed with red Valentine's hearts, because he had laughingly complained that the women got better gifts!

His wife, Deb, works for me too. She loves our parties; we threw one for her when she became a grandmother. I thought that was a great idea—a grandmother baby shower!—probably because I love buying baby gifts. Although my sons are growing up too fast, it's going to be a while before I get to buy things for my grandchildren. (But when I do, watch out.)

When my assistant got engaged, she couldn't wear her engagement ring because it was too big. She's not a jewelry-type person like me, so she didn't know where to go to have it sized. So the next Valentine's Day, my gift to her was taking her ring to be sized so she could wear it. I know she enjoyed the effort I made to give her something special. I try to pay attention to my employees' lives, so I know how to show my appreciation the way it matters most to them.

And our parties—we've had some memorable celebrations! I've taken my staff to wine-tasting events and big fundraisers. For holidays—Christmas and Mother's Day—I host fancy dinners at my house or downtown restaurants. Naturally we have a giant party after the madness of Valentine's Day, to celebrate making it through another year. It's a tradition to meet at the same sports bar, and everyone comes—every employee including some temps, with their spouses and kids. We reserve all the tables and eat greasy comfort food. I bring berries for the waitresses and presents for everyone.

What this all adds up to is loyalty. My employees feel like family because they *are* family. They love their jobs. They love working as part of a team of positive people who produce good products and great service.

In the end, I believe that most people would rather receive praise than a raise. This isn't just good for them; it's good for you, their employer. Your employees aren't just happier—they are more productive, more creative, and more responsible when they feel appreciated.

I know we deserved those awards as "Best Place to Work."

A Berry Good Tip

When you own a business, it is easy to work, and work, and work some more, without hearing much in the way of appreciation. Your boss doesn't praise you, because you're the boss!

It's so important to appreciate yourself for your hard work, persistence, and creativity. Find a way—a concrete, meaningful way—to pat yourself on the back.

For years I've had a reward system specially designed to get me through Valentine's Day week. That week is physically and mentally grueling, and by the evening of February 14 I am exhausted. So I designated February 15 as *my* Valentine's Day, and I buy myself a wonderful gift in appreciation of the hard work I do. For the first ten years or so of the business, I bought myself a piece of jewelry, which got more expensive each year as the business grew. Then for a couple of years we were so successful that I bought myself a new car instead. My thriftiness meant I bought a new used car, but it was always a really nice one.

Lately I've been scheduling vacation time in the second half of February, and I spend it resting and doing fun things with my boys. They're growing up now, and I want to spend as much time as I can with them before they're off doing their own things. Besides, I don't need any more jewelry!

It doesn't matter what form your appreciation of yourself takes. You don't have to buy yourself an expensive present or take a vacation. You just have to ensure that you get the recognition you deserve and a concrete reminder of the good you do. You must take care of you, physically, mentally, and spiritually. If you keep yourself happy, then your family, friends, customers, and employees are going to be happy. It's really as simple as that.

****

Shari's Secret Recipe #5
Chocolate-Strawberry Pizzas

"Pizza" Dough

2¾ cups all-purpose flour
¾ cup Ghirardelli Brand Sweet Ground Chocolate
½ tsp. salt
1 tsp. baking powder
1 cup salted butter, softened
1½ cups packed dark brown sugar
2 large eggs
1½ tsp. vanilla extract
5 cups mini marshmallows

Toppings

1 cup heavy whipping cream (divided)
½ cup (3 oz.) sugar
1½ cups (9 oz.) semisweet chocolate chips
3 pt. fresh strawberries
1½ cups chocolate chips, melted on defrost mode in microwave
   for 3-minute segments, or 1½ cups chocolate syrup

For Dough: In medium bowl, stir together the flour, ground chocolate, salt, and baking powder until combined. Set aside. In a large bowl, beat together the butter and brown sugar with an electric mixer on medium-high speed until light and fluffy. Add the eggs and vanilla and beat until well combined. Scrape down the sides of the bowl if necessary to make sure the mixture is well blended. Add the flour mixture and stir just until combined. Remove dough from the bowl and divide into 2 portions. Wrap each piece in plastic wrap, forming a flat circle shape. Refrigerate for at least 2 hours. It's okay to make the dough the day before.

When you are ready to bake your crusts, position an oven rack in the center and preheat oven to 325 degrees. Line 2 baking sheets with parchment paper. Remove the circles of "pizza" dough from the refrigerator. Let sit at room temperature for 15 minutes. Roll out the dough on a clean, lightly floured surface to a ¼-inch thickness, similar to how you would roll out a regular pizza or piecrust. Place each formed crust onto its own prepared baking sheet. Bake 1 sheet in the center of the oven until set, about 15 minutes.

Remove from the oven and quickly spread half of the marshmallows (2½ cups) around in the center of the hot crust up to the outer 1-inch edge of the crust. Place under oven broiler for approximately 3 to 5 minutes or until marshmallows are melted and *lightly* browned. The gooey marshmallow layer takes the place of the gooey cheese in a traditional pizza. Place on a wire rack to cool completely.

Bake the remaining dough as above and then repeat with the remaining marshmallows.

For Toppings: To make ganache topping,* mix ½ cup cream and ½ cup sugar in saucepan. Heat to boiling and remove from stove. Stir in 1½ cups of chocolate chips until melted. Add remaining ½ cup cream. Stir until spreading consistency is established and ganache is cooled, about 15 minutes. Spread ganache over cool melted marshmallow layers, leaving outside 1 inch of marshmallow exposed.

Prepare strawberries by slicing off top green hulls. Then slice each strawberry in half lengthwise. After ganache has set (about 15 minutes), decoratively place the sliced strawberries (important: skin/seed side down) in a circular layered pattern around the outer edge of the pizzas and working your way into the center. Press the backs of the berries down into the ganache to keep them in place.

For a final decorative touch, lightly drizzle (or as we say, swizzle) melted chocolate or chocolate syrup over the finished pizzas or individual slices of this unique, fun, and yummy pizza pie! Serve promptly. Makes 2 medium pizzas.

Get creative and add some extra ingredients to the second pizza! How about adding a layer of melted peanut butter between the marshmallow and chocolate finish? Then add banana slices, cherries, whipped Cream, nuts, and/or sprinkles.

Tip: This pizza goes great with a big glass of milk or a glass of Shari's Grand Reserve Zinfandel wine!

*It is okay to substitute your favorite chocolate butter-cream frosting for ganache.

Chapter 6

Have Faith

Many people say that mangoes from the Philippines are the best in the world. I agree with them. Most of the mangoes exported to the U.S. are from Mexico, where they grow in abundance, but Philippine mangoes . . . well, all I can say is that the first mango I tasted was a Philippine mango, and I was spoiled from that point on. Did you know that there's even a Facebook page devoted to the Philippine mango? It's full of yearning posts from expatriate Filipinos trying to describe their national fruit.

But Mexicans love their mangoes too. A few years ago, Clay and I vacationed in Manzanillo, Mexico. We flew in late at night, and by the time we were in the taxi on the way to our resort hotel, most of the countryside was totally dark. I asked the taxi driver if mangoes were in season, because I was already dreaming of breakfast the next morning.

"Si, it is perfect mango season," he said. "I'll take you somewhere right now." He turned the taxi around and began driving deeper into the countryside.

"Oh, no, that's all right," I protested. But the driver kept saying, "Oh, you must taste these; they are perfect." I guess he knew another mango-lover when he saw one.

He turned into a dirt road that ran through a mango farm. When we got to the hacienda, the driver hopped out and woke up the owner of the farm! The two of them went into the orchard with a flashlight, picked about fifteen mangoes off the trees, and gave them to me. Then the farm owner went back to bed, and the taxi driver drove us to our resort, as if they had done nothing special. I ate every one of those mangoes over the rest of the week we were there, and they were indescribably delicious. I think I tipped that taxi driver more than I ever tipped anyone before or since.

It's so hard to describe a taste in words. Mangoes are a slimy, slippery fruit, with a faint taste of turpentine beneath the perfect sweetness. But although slimy, slippery, and especially turpentine don't sound like positive attributes, with mangoes they are.

Mangoes are not that easy to eat because of that sliminess. Once you peel off the tough outer skin, they slide right off your knife. And your knife can get slippery too from all the juice dripping down—no, pouring down like an orange river. Pay attention or you might lose a finger. At the least you'll probably get your clothes messy and your face, arms, and hands all sticky, but after all you can wash your clothes and your face. Besides, you won't even care how primitive you look drenched in mango juice, because the feel of a mango sliding down your throat is worth it.

But in mango-loving cultures, they've discovered a way to eat a mango that will keep you at least semidry. Take a ripe mango, and slice off the fat "cheeks" of both sides of the mango, leaving the big pit in the middle. Take one of the cheeks and score a tic-tac-toe pattern into the flesh, cutting to the skin, but not through it. Hold the cheek in your hand and press the skin with your thumbs, turning the slice inside out to make a mango fan. Now you can scoop off the chunks with a spoon and place them into a bowl, if you're feeling civilized. If you're not, simply hold the slice up to your mouth and bite the sweet and easy chunks off with your teeth. This latter way means you will get your face messy, but again, so what?

* * * *

I'm often asked how I got to be so gutsy. It makes me laugh, because I know I'm not gutsy, not really. I worry, fret, and doubt myself, and sometimes I'm totally freaked out, just like everyone else.

It's true that when I started my business I had no fear, but that had more to do with youthful excitement coupled with ignorance. I was excited to be able to do something fun for a living instead of plod through mortgages or stocks, plus I was ignorant of just how hard it is to run your own business.

I have tender feelings—way too tender. If somebody doesn't smile at me, I think they don't like me. I hate having to defend myself from criticism. I take it personally, even though I know I shouldn't. As long as I can be prepared and organized, I can stand up for myself, but if I'm caught off-guard I nearly sink into the ground. I wish I had thicker skin, but I don't. I could never be a lawyer or a politician.

I would be a gooey melted mess in no time, just like chocolate after three minutes in the microwave.

And yet, I know you have to take some risks to achieve some gain. If you're too afraid to ask for what you want, you sure won't get it. I know that you can't quit just because you feel hurt. I know that being brave doesn't mean you have no fear—in fact, it's only courage if you are afraid. I have to remind myself quite often that I know these things.

We all have doubts and fears. It's how you handle them that makes or breaks you. Sometimes dealing with fear both makes *and* breaks you. I've learned that the key to dealing with doubt and fear is pretty simple; it's trust. Trust yourself, and more importantly, have faith in something or someone bigger than yourself.

Also trust your stomach.

Throwing Up

I have an unfortunate tendency to feel as though I'm going to throw up when I am scared or anxious, especially the anxiety that comes with being judged. At cheerleader tryouts when I was a senior in high school, I was sure I was going to throw up in front of the whole student body. I didn't, but only because I had nothing in my stomach. I made the squad but I bet I wouldn't have if anyone had known how terrified I was while performing my routine!

Probably the gutsiest thing I did as a kid was go to the Philippines as an exchange student when I was fifteen. I don't think I realized how gutsy it was until I got there, though—gutsy in more ways than one.

I'd always been a mama's girl. I wouldn't stay the night at a friend's house until I was at least twelve, and even as a teenager I wanted my friends to stay at my house instead. It's no wonder my parents were surprised when I told them I wanted to travel to the other side of the world by myself. I surprised myself. But I felt something "inside" telling me I should do this, and I trusted it even though I didn't understand it.

When I got off the airplane in Manila, clutching my three-by-five snapshot of the family that was supposed to meet me, I was greeted by what looked like thousands of people clustered around the entry area, and they all looked exactly like the people in my photo. I knew I would never find them and I'd be stuck in a foreign country all alone. My stomach started to churn. It didn't help that it was 100 percent humidity and ninety-five degrees on the tarmac, and I was wearing a suit with a long-sleeved jacket.

Eventually my Filipino family found me, thank God. We drove to a picnic where all the exchange students and their new families could meet. We were given Filipino-style clothes, shoes and everything, and then we sat down to eat. I had always been a picky eater. I didn't like rice. I hated all vegetables. I liked my meat well done. We were served a dish that wobbled like gelatin, but it was clear with no flavor. Then I watched while they buried a pig and sliced its throat, catching the blood in a pan. They warmed up the blood and then poured it over the gelatin stuff, rice, and vegetables on my plate. I could feel my stomach rising up. The mother of my new family was a tiny thing but she had a big personality. "You eat! You eat!" she cried, with her face about two inches from mine. I just shook my head. I knew I would die if I couldn't go home right away.

When we finally left the picnic, we drove to their house. They were a wealthy family, but on the way to their house we drove on pot-holed dirt roads through slums where people were living in cardboard boxes. I had never seen poverty like that. I was shocked and sad, but to be honest I was mostly scared. I didn't want to be anywhere near those slums.

At the house, which was a mansion by any standards, I was too miserable to notice anything. To get to our bedroom (I was sharing with the two daughters of the house) we had to climb a long flight of stairs. I was carrying my American clothes, including my suit jacket. Suddenly I knew I wasn't going to make it—I was going to throw up. I did. I held my jacket in front of me and threw up in it, the whole time I was climbing the stairs. I'm sure the maids were just thrilled with the new houseguest.

For the next two days, I lay in bed crying for my mother. But eventually it dawned on me that this place wasn't so bad. The mother who had told me to eat at the picnic was actually sweet to me while I was being such a pain. She still tried to get me to eat. On the third morning, I asked her if I could have bacon and eggs for breakfast instead of fish and rice, which is what they always ate. (Ugh.) Her face lit up. When I came down to breakfast, bacon and eggs were waiting for me. Even though the bacon was coated in a sugary gloss, the eggs were perfect, and for the rest of the time I lived there—three months—I had bacon and eggs for breakfast every morning. After the first morning, they served my bacon without the glaze, although I'm sure they thought I had strange tastes.

I think bacon and eggs cured my homesickness. I did learn to love most Filipino food, except for the warmed-up blood. I will never forget the taste of the amazing marinated meats they served, but best of all were the mangoes. I had never eaten mangoes before, and they became my second-favorite food, next to strawberries.

It wasn't just the food—I learned to love everything about the Philippines. The father of my family was a tobacco planter with many farms, and as we toured the Philippines I learned about the country. We even got caught in a typhoon once, stranding us in Baguio. It was scary and exciting at the same time. The group that sponsored the exchange program is called Youth for Understanding. We went to classes twice a week to learn about Filipino culture, and in return we shared our understanding of American culture with Filipino teenagers.

Being teenagers, we also had a lot of fun. For one thing, there were few restrictions based on age. I was treated like an adult, which is a pretty heady thing for a fifteen-year-old. I went out on dates with boys approved by Youth for Understanding, nearly all of whom had a Mercedes. Disco was "in" and the movie *10* with Bo Derek had just come out. I decided to get my hair done like hers, in cornrows. And I didn't have to ask permission!

My cornrowed hair sure caused my mom's eyebrows to go up when she and Ben picked me up at the airport in San Francisco three months later. But she said nothing. They wanted to take me out to a nice dinner, but I insisted we go to McDonald's for a real American burger. For me, culture is all in the food.

I am so glad I showed my guts by listening to my gut, even though I literally spilled my guts at first. That trip to the Philippines opened my eyes to the big world waiting outside my small one. For all I know, I might never have left Klamath Falls without it.

Enjoying myself as an exchange student in the Philippines (sophomore year 1980).

Trust in the Positive

When I first told people about my strawberry business idea, the response was usually silence. I saw raised eyebrows and rolled eyes when they thought I wasn't looking. Even my closest friends and family—Clay, my mom, my sister, Grannie—weren't sure about the idea. It's not that they didn't support me, because they did. They just thought they'd better stick close by me so they could help me pick myself up when I fell on my face.

I can't really blame them. Planning to dip strawberries in chocolate as a business was a little out there. I knew that no bank would give me a loan to start such a business, and in fact I never even considered trying to get one. Too many people had already told me that my idea would never work.

However, as a stockbroker I belonged to a networking group, and in that group was a Mary Kay consultant. I loved Mary Kay products, but more than that, I loved Mary Kay herself. I read everything I could find about her, because her story affirmed my dream. She was also told that her cosmetics business idea would never work. The numbers didn't add up, said the accountants. She was told she couldn't have both a family and a career; she had to choose. She couldn't get a bank loan, so she used her modest savings as startup capital. She was a master of scheduling her time, just like me. Above all, she knew how to market, promote, and sell, which I knew were my greatest talents as well. Because Mary Kay Cosmetics was an enormous international success, these similarities gave me the courage to believe in my idea.

I love that the symbol Mary Kay used to launch her business was the bumblebee. It's the perfect symbol for women in business, because all the experts agree that the bumblebee should not be able to fly—and yet it does. Women were told for centuries that we could not succeed in business and still raise a family, but we do.

You will always find people who will tell you it (whatever "it" may be) can't be done. That was true for Mary Kay, and it was true for me. You don't have to choose between your family and your career. You just have to set your priorities and get yourself organized.

I didn't listen to the discouraging voices. I was too busy with so much work to do and didn't have time for any negative energy.

When I started the original Shari's Bear'ys, I figured that as long as I could pay for my rent, car, and groceries and have a little fun once in a while, I was going to make it.

It was the same story when I expanded my business and opened a retail store—most people thought I was making a mistake. There was a small nail and hair salon just three doors down from my new store. The owners came into the store one day while we were still building and painting walls in preparation for our grand opening. I was a nervous wreck because there was so much to do, and although I was pretending to be brave, I have to admit I had a few doubts. What if I really was making a mistake? Maybe no one would come to my store—how embarrassing that would be!

"What are you going to sell?" asked one of the nail-salon owners, Vivian.

"Chocolate-dipped strawberries," I said.

"What else?"

"Just chocolate-dipped strawberries."

"Oh," she said, looking at me with kindly pity, as if she thought I was mentally challenged. As they left, I heard her mutter under her breath, "Poor thing, she's never going to make it."

About two months later, during my first Valentine's Day at my new store, the line to get in stretched all down the shopping center, a long way past the nail salon's windows. Traffic was a mess because people were pulling over just to see what everyone else was pulling over for. The local TV stations sent camera crews out to capture the chaos on film.

Vivian became one of my best friends and most ardent supporters. Now when I have a new idea, she never even questions it. "Oh, you'll find a way to make it work," she says.

Trust Your Experience

I'm not well educated. Clay; my right-hand person, Glenda; and in fact a lot of people tease me about being an Archie Bunker. I often say words wrong. Sometimes Clay will stand next to me and whisper the right words to me before I can mess them up. "Don't even try to use big words," they tell me.

I've accepted that this is just who I am. I don't worry about it much anymore, because even though I'm not super educated, I have good instincts. Above all, I don't mind hard work. That's been enough for me to succeed.

School was not something I loved. My parents didn't push it, none of my grandparents even finished high school, and I was the first person in my family to attend college at all. And I was only there to buy time until I figured out what I was going to do. I've always been more of a "street smarts" girl, learning in the real world rather than in a lecture hall or from reading a book. (And here I am writing one!)

I managed to get good grades through high school and college, but if I'm going to be honest, I have to admit I sort of gamed the system sometimes. I made it a point to become friends with my teachers; I found out what they liked and didn't like. I helped them by doing the things they didn't like. And I gave them things they did—just as I still do when I take my boys' teachers some chocolate-dipped strawberries. It worked. I graduated with a two-year associate of arts degree. Once in a while you need to go through the back door to get to where you're going. I'm really bad at following rules. Sometimes it's okay to break them.

I don't boast about my lack of education. I now wish I had taken courses in general business and accounting. I wish I'd taken courses in computer skills. But I know enough to understand which experts I should hire to help me.

However, my lack of formal business education does sometimes contribute to doubts about myself. When I was working in my national Shari's Berries company, I worked closely with someone who was very proud of his degree, and he continually reminded me that I didn't have one. It was hurtful, and when the new CEO began changing the direction of the company, I didn't fight it as much as I should because he was so sure he was right and I was wrong. I mean, who was I, anyway? I felt that in his eyes I was just a little hick girl with a basket of strawberries and no college degree. It is surprising how easy it is to let others' opinions about you invade your thinking. Luckily I didn't let those opinions hang around forever.

Whenever I start to doubt myself because of my lack of education, I think of what William Lyon Phelps, who was the president of Yale University, once said. "I believe in a university education for

Easter Sunday with my sister, Dayna. She was six and I was three.

My Klamath Union High School senior yearbook, featuring me on the cover, cheering on the crowd.

With my sister, Dayna, and stepfather, Ben (1979).

June 1982, at my high-school graduation, with Clay—my dream man . . .

On Venice Beach, California, in June of 1985, when Ben escorted me to Los Angeles, where I would be starting a new chapter of my life.

Mom painting my bear logo on the wall of my first store on Auburn Boulevard in Sacramento. The store and logo are still there today under my Berry Factory brand!

Holding my first son, Paxton, in front of my first store. (Note: He's in a strawberry suit—the only boy who would have a reason to wear such an outfit!)

My boys and me playing in chocolate and strawberries during a fun photo shoot. As my business grew, so did my family. I love to include them whenever possible! Paxton, Max (in my lap), and Hogan (behind me; notice his broken arm . . . very typical).

Clay and me on our wedding day, April 11, 1992. Dreams do come true!

Serving 350 dipped berries at 30,000 feet (between Vegas and New York City), living out one of my old dreams of being a flight attendant!

Doing Vanna's job on "Wheel of Fortune."

How my place on the wheel looks today!

Celebrating my fortieth birthday, a chauffeured day of wine tasting (in my neighborhood) for me and thirty-two of the most important people in my life. (I was teased that I was in mourning, so I went for the "Jackie O" look, which included a black veil over my face.) Left to right: Mom, Emily, me, Glenda.

With my best friend, Gena, spinning "Wheel of Fortune"'s big wheel on a special taping for NBA week (in New York City onstage at Radio City Music Hall).

Hogan and Max working at our California State Fair booth with Olympian Ruthie Bolton.

Vacationing with my boys, Hogan, Max, and Paxton. It's my favorite thing to do!

Clay and me celebrating with Grannie at her ninetieth birthday party in Las Vegas.

Son Paxton and me at a PAWS fundraiser with Alec Baldwin.

With Willie Nelson on his bus. Every time I see this picture, I think, "Why didn't I braid my hair?"

With Kathy Ireland, in L.A. at Jennifer Openshaw's Women in the Millionaire Zone conference, where we both were speakers.

Dipping treats in chocolate at school with my son Max, another annual tradition I have with my boys.

In Lake Tahoe in 2007 with Dad and Max Baer, Jr. (aka Jethro Bodine from the 1960s series "The Beverly Hillbillies").

With Sacramento mayor Kevin Johnson (2008).

My first magazine cover (February 2007)!

Mom cookin' it up with Guy Fieri and a bottle of my Zinfandel wine!

Hanging out with Erik Estrada at Red Hawk Casino's celebrity night.

Holding a bouquet of my patented strawberry roses while posing at a photo shoot with my mascot, Miss Swizzle.

My most popular gift box, a one-dozen fancy assortment.

With sons Hogan and Max during a tour of the Jelly Belly® factory.

This is how "Berried in Chocolate" really looks!

I'll do almost anything to sell a strawberry! Here I am with my candy-cane-flavored berries posing for a Christmas postcard (2006).

both men and women," he said, "but I believe a knowledge of the Bible without a college course is more valuable than a college course without the Bible."

And guess what . . . I have learned the value and great benefit of trusting God and His Word, the Bible, in all my decisions.

Trust in God

I was born and raised a Catholic. Grannie and everyone on her side of the family were devout Catholics. My mom's aunt, Grannie's sister-in-law, had many children. She was so strict with them that on Sundays they weren't allowed to brush their teeth before going to church, because she believed that you are not supposed to eat or drink anything before communion and was afraid they'd swallow toothpaste.

After my grandfather died, Grannie said the Rosary every single day until the day she died. When she was in her nineties, she'd often fall asleep in the middle of saying it. But she kept her fingers on the beads even while asleep, so she'd know where to start up again once she awoke!

My faith has always been a big part of who I am. I learned early that Jesus is God in the flesh. As a little girl I was taught about giving, forgiving, tithing, and not holding onto the things of this world too tightly. I learned that I am here on earth for a reason.

I am grateful for the lessons I learned in the Catholic Church, but today I call myself a Christian. I once heard a metaphor that describes going to church this way: "Sitting in a church pew doesn't make you a Christian any more than sitting in a garage makes you a car!"

A few years before I got married, when I was still Shari of Shari's Bear'ys, I was a featured speaker for a Christian Women's Luncheon group. Joy Moore was in charge of the "entertainment" (me). She later became one of my dearest friends and earliest employees. Joy is a Christian and her favorite thing is leading others to know Jesus.

Joy invited me to her Bible study group. I wanted to go because although the Bible had always interested me, I had never owned one. Joy helped me understand what it meant to be a Christian and encouraged me to know Jesus personally. Several months later in my home, during a private Bible study with Joy, she read aloud Romans 10:9-10, "For if you confess with your mouth that Jesus is Lord and believe in your heart that God raised him from the dead, you will be saved. For it is by believing in your heart that you are made right with God, and it is by confessing with your mouth that you are saved."

She then asked me if I was ready. And oh was I! I felt that I had been ready all my life. All these years I had Jesus in my head but not in my heart! I was missing heaven by eighteen inches—the space between my head and my heart. I learned that praying is our way of talking to God directly and that reading the Bible is His way of talking to us. Now Jesus is the High Priest and is the mediator between us and God. It's all right there in the Bible.

Can you imagine a popular book (or *anything* that is popular) today that will still be popular 2,000 years from now? Probably not. But the Bible is still the number-one bestseller in the world. It is old yet it is ever new.

Clay grew up in a Christian home but did not have a personal relationship with Jesus. He didn't go to church except when he'd go with me on Christmas and Easter. It wasn't until our first son, Paxton, was born that Clay became a Christian. We almost lost Paxton immediately after he was born. That day God healed not only my baby's sickness but gave Clay a new heart as well. During two difficult weeks, I got to witness the amazing power of prayer. Within a year, Clay was leading a Bible study in our home. Today my Wednesday morning Bible study group is one of my favorite places to go. Clay is also a Youth Leader at our church, and the kids all love him. Probably because he's a big kid himself.

Trusting My Faith

Why am I talking about Jesus in a book about business success? Because years ago I dedicated my business to God. That is the main reason it is so magical. I mean, it's only chocolate-dipped strawberries, for goodness sake! I'm not the first one to make them or the only one selling them. But right from the beginning things have fallen into place for me. Yes, I had to work hard and plan well, but I know that without God's blessing, none of this magical mystery ride would have happened.

I believe that God chose this business for me. He has a plan for my life, and it's up to me to trust Him that His way will be best. I'm able to keep a positive attitude because I know that God is working in my life. God's plan for me and my business has not always been easy or the way I envisioned it. But I know that He is in charge and all that He does is for my good. This peace that "passes all understanding" has guided me in all my business endeavors and has enabled me to be understanding and patient in my dealings with my customers and employees. It has encouraged me to give back to the community and be appreciative of all that God has given me.

I know that my life will have its hardships no matter what, but I also know that God will be there to help me through. Faith doesn't solve your problems; it just gives you strength to weather them. Christianity doesn't promise an easy life. But it gives you great tools to live a good one.

The best tool of all, of course, is God's Word. I now keep a journal. I wish I had kept one sooner, because it really helps to clear my mind so I can hear what God is whispering to me. One of my favorite scripture verses is about trust, from Proverbs 3:5-6. It was the first one I ever memorized and I come back to it again and again: "Trust in the Lord with all your heart; do not lean on your own understandings. In all your ways acknowledge Him and He will direct your paths."

Prayer and meditation on God's Word help me make decisions, both for my family and my business. In decision making, it's important to distinguish between our emotions and what we know to be true. The truth found in the Bible must always override our feelings. Prayer makes this easier for me. I've learned that my timing and God's timing are not the same. It says in James 1:5, "If you need wisdom, ask God, and He will gladly tell you." But James does not say *when* God will tell you. It's part of developing your "faith muscle" to have faith that the answer *will* come, in God's time.

I am a natural-born worrier. Clay says I worry whenever the wind blows. (He never worries about anything, which is sometimes a little irritating.) Worry is one of the reasons I work so hard—so that I'll be too busy to worry!

When I'm distracted by worry, I remember that worry is accepting responsibility that God never intended us to have, as it says in 1 Peter 5:7: "Cast all your worry upon Him because he cares for you." I also learned a great method for dealing with worry from Kelvin Boston, a wise man whom I met when we were speakers on a panel together at a recent conference. He said to make a list of all the things that cause you anxiety—bills, lack of sales, the war, the stock market, your kid's grades, the rash you just got on your hands, whatever. Then sort this big list into three new lists. The first list contains all the things you can do something about. Then do something about that list, such as help your kid with his homework. The second list contains the things you need help with. Then get the help you need, such as hiring a financial consultant or going to the doctor for that rash. And the third list contains the things you can't do anything about, such as the war and the stock market. Those are the things you pray about. You leave them in God's hands and move on.

My church pastor's wife, WilleJune, has been helping me with worry too. Have you ever noticed that worry is always focused on tomorrow and what's *going* to happen? WilleJune recently told me that she thinks I need to meditate on a line from the Lord's Prayer: "Give us this day our daily bread." Our *daily* bread. We don't own tomorrow. We can't control it; only God can. We can only claim today. In other words, "Let go and let God."

Speaking Your Truth

Many people have criticized me for how vocal I am about my faith. Although Joy shared the good news with me and it's so much a part of who I am, these criticisms have hurt. But in prayer I take them to my heavenly Father and give them to Him. As a Christian, it is important for me to share my faith with others—how it has helped me grow and live a good life. How would I spread God's message of love if I only hung out with people who already know about it? I want people to see that I am happy and full of fun and generosity. Who knows, maybe they'll be curious about what makes me so. If that happens, great. It gives me the opportunity to share my awesome God and what He can also do for them. But it's not up to me. Only God can save. I'm happy to be His servant here on earth.

Most people have heard of the Serenity Prayer, which begins with the famous lines, "God grant me the serenity to accept the things I cannot change, the courage to change the things I can, and the wisdom to know the difference." But not everyone knows that this prayer is much longer, and the rest of the words are just as beautiful and full of meaning. I have memorized this prayer and repeat parts of it to myself every day. It gets me through those times when my feelings have been hurt or I'm worrying about something I can do nothing about.

The Serenity Prayer

God grant me the serenity
To accept the things I cannot change,
The courage to change the things I can,
And the wisdom to know the difference.

Living one day at a time,
Enjoying one moment at a time,
Accepting hardship as the pathway to peace.

Taking, as He did, this sinful world
As it is, not as I would have it;
Trusting that He will make all things
Right if I surrender to His will;

That I may be reasonably happy
In this life,
And supremely happy with Him
Forever in the next.

The Brave Mom

My son Hogan once had an essay to write at school, the topic being himself—kind of like a mini-autobiography. Hogan showed me his paper. He wrote about how his parents taught him to think for himself and not be afraid. In the next paragraph, he wrote how fun his dad was to hang around with and how he knew how to fix anything that was broken. In the third paragraph, he wrote about me and how I always knew what to do. He started off the paragraph with the sentence, "My mom is so brave."

This is the very best compliment I have ever been given.

A Berry Good Tip

You know a fake when you see one. If you have doubts about yourself, think you're too this or not enough that, don't ever pretend to be anything other than who you are. In fact, you can take the things you think are "wrong" or "strange" about you and make them part of your brand. Make who you are work for you.

I like glitz and glitter. When I show up at events, I emphasize my big hair and wear bright colors and gaudy jewelry. I know it's not everyone's style, but it's my style and always has been. Now people expect to see me looking "like me." They know they're seeing the real Shari.

When I do speaking gigs, I talk about my faith as well as the other factors of my success. I know there will be people in the audience who are not Christian; maybe there are some who are anti-religious. I'm not there to make them uncomfortable, but if I did not mention the most important thing in my life, I would not be me. And I am who they came to hear speak.

When I opened my first retail store, I had a bright idea for a tagline to put on a banner across our window. I wanted to emphasize that our chocolate-covered berries were an alternative to sending flowers, so it read: *Edible Florist.* It wasn't long before someone told me that my sign was causing some ridicule because it wasn't grammatically correct. The sign was actually saying you could buy chocolate-covered florists and eat them. Some radio DJs got hold of it, and the next time I went on the radio, the DJs had a lot of fun teasing me.

My attitude was: "Hey, whatever gets attention!" I told people that I often made mistakes like that, unintentionally mixing up words so they came out sounding funny or weird. This is just another part of who I am.

During one uncomfortable SBI board meeting, it was announced that they didn't think it was good to have a live person be the brand. I believe that this was a mistake. They left a lot of magic on the table when they got rid of the "real Shari." People want to know there's a real, live person behind the products and services they're buying. Why else do you think every company these days has a blog on their Web site? Your customers want to know the real you, big hair and all.

****

Shari's Secret Recipe #6
Mango Pie

Pie

1 3-oz. pkg. peach (or orange or apricot) flavored gelatin, regular or sugar free
¾ cup mango nectar (find in juice or ethnic-food aisle), divided
4 cups sliced and peeled ripe mango (about 4 medium mangoes)
1 piecrust (see recipe in chapter 2), cooked and cooled

My Mom's Fresh Whipped Cream

½ pt. heavy whipping cream
¼ cup sugar
1 tbsp. vanilla

For Pie: Combine gelatin and 2 tbsp. mango nectar in large microwave-safe bowl. Let stand 5 minutes. Microwave on high for 15 seconds. Stir and microwave for an additional 15 minutes or until gelatin dissolves. Stir in remaining mango nectar; chill in refrigerator 5 minutes. Add mango pieces, stirring gently to separate slices and evenly coat with gelatin mixture. Spoon mango mixture into piecrust. Cover and chill approximately 4 hours or until gelatin is set.

For Whipped Cream: Use a *metal* bowl! Chill bowl and beater in fridge before you whip the cream. Whip cream with electric beater until thickened, then slowly add the sugar and vanilla. Beat until soft-peak stage. Note: Don't overwhip the cream, which will make it curdle. Spread over entire top of pie and serve.

Tip: Perfectly ripe mangoes are the key to this recipe. The best time of year for mangoes is normally June and July. They should have some yellow and/or red on them. Try not to buy hard, green mangos. They should have a sweet smell when you buy them. Most times you need to buy the mangoes 3 to 4 days ahead of time and let them ripen on the kitchen counter. A mango is ready to eat when it yields slightly to gentle pressure.

Chapter 7

Start

Ooh, fresh cherries. Dark red skin stretched so tight over sweet flesh; maroon cherry juice running down your chin as you suck the fruit off the pit. They would be even better dipped in chocolate, right?

Well, no, because of that darn pit. It just gets too messy, and besides, what if a customer bit down and broke a tooth? There doesn't seem to be any way to de-pit them that won't break the fresh cherry apart. I know because I've tried, and tried.

I guess I could have found a way to do it if I wanted to sink a bunch of money into research, but another problem with cherries is that you can't get them all year round. I didn't want to spend time and effort on something I can only do one or two months out of the year.

But then I remembered that way back when I was making baskets for realtors, if I couldn't get good strawberries (this was before I was the strawberry queen with unbeatable sources), I did dip cherries—maraschino cherries.

Now I'm doing this again, and this time I have a name: Cherry Babies. (It's a play on my name, get it? Doesn't it make you want to sing, "Cher-er-ry, cherry baby"?)

I take a cluster of three maraschino cherries, twist the stems together, dip them in dark, milk, or white chocolate, then decorate with a contrasting swizzle. The creamy chocolate contrasts perfectly with the texture of the maraschino cherries.

And now I have figured out how to make chocolate-dipped fresh cherries without the pit. I recently launched them as part of my new frozen line of gourmet dipped fruits. Find them in the frozen food aisle at your favorite grocer!

****

Many people come up and talk to me after I give speeches. They want to know my "secrets" on how to start a business. (As I've said before, I don't have any secrets!) I've found that the people seeking this kind of advice usually fall into one of two categories, both of which break my heart.

The first kind are those who talk themselves out of following their dreams because they don't have enough money, or they don't know the right people, or they don't know accounting or business or computers or what-have-you. The second kind are those who quit their nine-tofive jobs, mortgage their homes, or drain their retirement funds before they find out if their ideas are feasible or even fun. The first kind barely sticks their toes in the water before yanking them back out because the water feels cold. The second kind jumps right in the deep end before they learn how to swim. Neither of these strategies works very well.

Start Small, but Start

My answer to both kinds of people is the same: go ahead and start your business, yet start on a small scale. You don't have to have a lot of money, and you don't have to do everything big and splashy and perfect right off the bat. In fact, you *can't* do everything perfect off the bat—because you won't know enough yet. First learn the ropes before you move on to the next stage. Maybe you can start with your friends and family using your product or service, and then branch out to *their* friends and families. Make your initial offering a small one, maybe just one product or service. Keep your inventory as low as possible. Use word of mouth advertising, the cheapest but still the best marketing tool around. This will give you some time to get the bugs out, get your pricing and other systems working correctly, and get some cash flow going before you quit your nine-to-five job.

Before you jump into your own business, make sure you've done this job before and know what it's like. For example, if you love to cook and entertain and you have this great idea for an innovative restaurant that you just know will take off like a rocket, but you have never worked in a restaurant before, you might be heading for disaster if you don't get some real-time restaurant experience. Get a job as a waitperson, cashier, or dishwasher and learn how a restaurant runs.

My five-dollar-an-hour job as a delivery person before I started Shari's Bear'ys taught me lessons that prevented a ton of mistakes later on.

Besides, what if you take out a huge loan to start your great new business and then discover that you just hate running a business? I wanted to be a stewardess when I was young, but boy am I glad now I didn't get hired. I wanted the prestige of working in the financial world, but as a stockbroker I was bored. I'm glad I didn't go into debt pursuing either one of these dreams.

So start small, but do start. Invest in business cards and start building your dream, block by block. You have to try. Don't just leave it as a dream. You'll kick yourself later if you don't try. You'd never know how it could have been. Those are such sad words, *could have been.*

Follow the Money

I've always been a risk-taker, but at the same time I don't risk more than I can afford to lose. I love to play video poker machines, just like my Grannie—and I seem to have inherited her luck too, so I'm in no danger of being buried by gambling debts. A primary reason for my success is that I balance my risk-taking with caution, especially with money. I can still hear Grannie telling me, "Count your pennies and the dollars will take care of themselves."

That reminds me of a story my dad told me. He has a huge yard, and it's hot in southern Oregon in the summer. He complains about having to mow his big yard. One day, he went out to mow and noticed that the kids across the street had set up a lemonade stand. Their sign read: *Lemonade: 10 cents. All You Can Drink.*

Dad thought, "That's a pretty good deal. When I'm done mowing, I'll get a dime and go over there and take advantage of it." So when he was done, he went across the street and gave the kids his dime. They poured lemonade into one of those little Dixie cups, like you'd have in the bathroom. He quickly washed it down, put down the empty cup, and said, "I'll have some more."

One of the kids replied, "That'll be another dime, sir."

Dad said, "Wait a minute. Your sign says: ten cents, all you can drink."

The kid looked him straight in the eye and said, "Yes, and for ten cents, that's all you can drink."

Dad always laughs when he tells this story. I sometimes wonder what happened to those kids. Did they grow up to be entrepreneurs?

I read that one of Warren Buffett's rules is to always spell out the deal before you start the work. This is one of my rules too. You can get a better deal if you ask for it ahead of time rather than afterward. It's like buying a car—once you drive off the lot, you're not going to get any extras. If you want those extras, you'd better ask for them before you sign on the dotted line.

There are people who call me a tightwad—and they are probably right. After all, I was trained by Ben, who was the King of the Tightwads. I'm proud to be like him and proud of my ability to get value for my money. I know how to get good deals if they're there to be gotten. And if I want something that costs more than I can afford, I can often figure out a creative way to get it anyway, or at least an excellent substitute.

Sometimes charm works. In the beginning, while I was still working out of my apartment, I found a wonderful chocolate supplier, a wholesaler in San Francisco. Their chocolate was to die for—rich, dark, luscious, and the perfect texture for strawberry dipping. The problem was that their minimum order was 500 pounds. That was way beyond my financial capacity, not to mention physical capacity of my tiny kitchen! *But I wanted their chocolate.* So I called them from a phone booth on my lunch break (I was working for the balloon delivery company at the time), and I managed to get their sales manager on the phone. The upshot was that they allowed me to buy only 200 pounds for my first order. And no, I didn't do anything illegal or unethical. I just convinced them that if they'd allow me to buy below their minimum just this one time, I would become a great customer in the future. I'd guesstimate that over the last twenty years, my companies have purchased well over two million pounds of their products. I bet they're glad they took a risk with me.

I was home-based for the first two years of the business. I didn't have much capital. I couldn't get an SBA loan because my business wasn't at least two years old, and I had no collateral. I don't blame the banks; they have rules that make sense. I was willing to start small and prove myself. As it turned out, I didn't need an SBA loan after all. For the first nine years of my business, I borrowed no money and built the business using my profits only.

I continued working out of my tiny apartment, saving my pennies and building the business brick by brick, until my business became too "busy" to work out of my home safely. You see, I was supposed to be licensed as a commercial food vendor, and for that I had to have a commercially licensed kitchen. That was something I wasn't able to afford.

I kept my kitchen scrupulously clean, but an anonymous health-department employee told me that a jealous competitor had reported that I was working out of my home. Within twenty-four hours, I moved my business out of my house and set up production space in a commercial kitchen. I was able to do that so quickly due to paying attention to opportunities. About a year before, I'd met a guy at one of the Sacramento food festivals; John and I had adjoining display booths. He was the owner of a restaurant. We hit it off, and sometime during the festival he told me that he had extra space in his restaurant, with a walk-in refrigerator and everything. It wasn't being used, so he said, "If you ever need extra space, give me a call."

I remembered him, called him, and went to see him at his restaurant that same day. He said, "Sure," and we made a deal. I went home, loaded up my Chevy Blazer, and was set up in my new space the next day. Then I applied for a license and worked out of that space for six months until I got my first store.

When I meet women now who want to open a food business, I tell them this story and advise them to do something similar—only do it *before* you open up! One good idea is to find a donut shop. They're usually open from 3:00 a.m. until noon; then they're closed and their kitchens are empty. Maybe you could make a deal to work there in the late afternoons while your business grows. And these days you can find "catering kitchens" for rent, sometimes even by the hour. You'd have a licensed place to work in, and when you're ready, you can move to your own place. This strategy worked for me.

When I did open my first store in 1991, it wasn't in a prime, high-rent location. I picked a centrally located place with easy freeway access, which is critical for quick delivery. It was also where I could negotiate a good lease. All my expansions since then have been fiscally prudent too. I didn't open more stores than I could afford or support. I never wanted to create debt. To me, debt is public enemy number one.

Just One Thing

You know that KISS saying, "Keep It Simple, Stupid"? It applies to starting a business too. Many people start a business and try to do too many things too fast. I think it's important in the beginning to keep your business simple and focused on one thing—then be the very best at that one thing. Or if your business or service is something common, pick out one unique thing about you, and focus on that.

You can't specialize in a bunch of things. If you did, they wouldn't be special, would they? When I started out, I offered catering services as well as chocolate-dipped berries. But it wasn't long before my energy was scattered, so I cut back as soon as I could to only offer my unique product. It made marketing my product so much easier, because my customers knew exactly what I offered.

When I did choose to expand, I was careful to add things slowly, and one at a time. I even learned to be patient, which was really hard for me. But it takes a while for a new product to get off the ground. For example, it took a couple of years for my idea of selling chocolate-dipped bottles of wine to really take off.

When you keep it simple at first, it allows you to gain the customer's trust and loyalty, and then you can let them know what else you can do.

This principle applies in areas other than business too. When I think of specializing and food, I often think of Clay. He is the BBQ king when we go camping, which we do often with our boys. Clay loves to wrap things in foil and place them on the coals to cook, turning the most mundane ingredients cooked the old-fashioned way into miraculous creations. You just haven't lived until you've had his version of Bananas Foster or his candied apples. At the end of this chapter, I'm sharing these recipes with you. I'm pretty sure he won't mind.

Throw That Spaghetti

Although it's a good idea to aim to be the best or most unique at one thing, marketing that one thing is different. Marketing is where you can let your creativity soar. My advice is to market your product or service in as many ways as you can afford. Try out different techniques to get the word out. Even the ideas that sound zany in the beginning may actually work, and if they don't, you'll probably learn something that does. If you can imagine it, there's the possibility of making it reality. To use yet another one of my favorite clichés, throw some spaghetti at the wall to see what sticks.

I had to use low-budget, seat-of-the-pants marketing to build my business, because I could not afford big billboards and high-profile advertising. I kept things simple by knowing what was going on in my market, which in the beginning was Sacramento. I had a simple goal, too: to expose as many people to my product as possible.

Every morning, my radio wakes me up to my favorite station. When my business was still in its incubator stage, I woke up every morning hearing the DJ giving away gifts, and I thought, "I bet that company is just trading their gifts for a mention on the air—I could do that!" And when I started Shari's Bear'ys, I did. The first marketing gig I did with the media was one morning about a week after I started my business. I got up at five o'clock to be live on the morning radio show. It was October, so we gave away Halloween-themed baskets full of strawberries decorated to look like jack-o-lanterns. They were so happy with the berries that they put me on the radio with the popular morning DJs, and we bantered back and forth while they munched on my berries. "You sure have some nice berries, Shari," they said, and I just played along. I had a blast, and even better, my phone started ringing.

Radio has been my favorite advertising method from then on. I gave berries away on the radio stations in exchange for air time and mentions and continue to do so today. Traditional advertising is so expensive, and in my experience you don't get the bang you should get for your buck. I get better results from advertising that is free than advertising I have to pay for.

Of course, it's not completely free—it costs me some strawberries and chocolate. And I learned that at some point you do need to put some cash in the pot, paying for some regular recorded advertising spots. You need to keep the sales department happy as well!

I didn't limit myself to the radio, either. When I was getting started, I read the newspaper every Monday morning to see which women's groups, community groups, or Chambers of Commerce were meeting that week, and if I could, I'd attend those meetings— with my strawberries, which I gave away for free. I figured if I could get people to taste the berries, they would remember me. You have to get your product or service "out there" so people will get accustomed to using it, especially a product like mine. Once you taste one, you've gotta have another, just like those potato chips! You have to give in order to receive, you know. It doesn't pay to be stingy. In my first year I'm pretty sure I gave away more berries than I sold.

My product is truly made for word-of-mouth advertising—in more ways than one. I joined networking lead groups when I was getting started, and they added their mouths to mine. Not only did they buy my berries and tell others about them, they gave me business advice and pat-on-the-back support when I needed it most.

I attended trade shows, arts and crafts fairs, home and garden shows, you name it—as long as an event featured food, I was there. When concerts came to Sacramento, I often sent a basket of berries to the performers, as a welcome gift. I partnered with local companies to offer my berries as prizes for contests they sponsored, on the radio or TV. Contests are great for providing name recognition, and the winners almost always become my loyal customers.

And everywhere I went, I gave away berries and business cards, and I collected the business cards of everyone I met, asking if I could put them on my mailing list. Within a year, I had 3,000 names on my list.

You need to be bold and take a risk when marketing. You don't know that Ted Nugent is going to call you the next day after you give him berries at a concert. You don't know that Halle Berry is going to become a customer if you send her berries. You don't know that Halle Berry will win an Oscar, either, and as a celebration gift she'll send berries to all her famous friends and connections. But if you don't try, she won't. You have to throw it up there. You have to use your imagination to create a new reality. Be a dreamer. That's what my chief operations officer Glenda calls me.

Who's This 'We'?

When I first started in 1989, I had one full-time employee: me. I did everything. I answered the phone; I made the product and delivered it; I bought all the components and did the bookkeeping; I did the cleanup. I was *it*, although I also employed two or three temporary seasonal employees, who just happened to be my family and friends. In 1991, when I opened my first store, I had two part-time production employees and a van, which I drove (I doubled as delivery girl). The seasonal temps continued to be friends and family. In 1994, I opened my second store and had six full-time production employees, a bookkeeper, and, yes, those same friendly temporary employees.

Although I grew slowly, I projected the image of a seasoned, professional, larger company. I didn't tell people I was just starting out and was all alone. I said, "We chocolate-dip strawberries and put them into decorated baskets, and then we deliver them directly to you." One time I was talking to my brother Rick, who used to be my boss when I was in the mortgage business. He asked me how I did something, and I said, "Well, we do this. . . . " He interrupted me by asking, "Who's this 'we'?"

I laughed, but I didn't stop saying "we." I tell others starting out to do the same thing. Go ahead—act bigger than you are. You'll make it come true soon enough.

Opportunities Abound

I never planned for my business to grow so fast and be as popular as it became. Most people write their business plan before they start. I'm sure that's good advice, but it's not what I did. I just followed opportunities as they came up. My experience has shown that there are always opportunities out there. Most people just don't see them, because they don't believe they are there.

I think one reason I've been successful is that I'm always on alert for those opportunities. Several years ago, Clay and I and the boys moved to our current home in the foothills outside Sacramento. My mom and stepdad, Ron, were helping us move. We'd spent an exhausting day unloading and unpacking the kitchen—I have a lot of kitchen stuff! At the end of the day, we were dirty and tired and very hungry. No one wanted to cook, that's for sure.

"Let's go out," I said. "I think I saw a restaurant down near the crossroads, where the post office and that little store are." I thought it was probably a local hangout, maybe a burger joint since the sign said *Grill*. But any place that served food would be fine with us.

I was wearing an old dirty T-shirt and tennis shoes, and my hair was pulled back in a ponytail. I had no makeup, of course. Mom didn't look much better. We were all so tired and hungry we didn't care.

We entered the restaurant, which is called the Gold Vine Grill, and immediately discovered it's a fine restaurant that wouldn't be out of place in Manhattan. It catered to the close-knit wine community, although I didn't know that then. The owners, Mary and Greg

Kemp, looked at us in all our grubbiness and didn't bat an eye. Mary showed us to a lovely table in the center of the restaurant and served us a fabulous gourmet meal, treating us as favored guests. She had no idea who I was, although at the end of the meal Ron asked her, "Do you know who this is?" and my grubby cover was blown.

I was so impressed with the service and the food that I wrote a review of the restaurant, which was published in *Sacramento Magazine*. Since then, Mary and I have become good friends. My review is framed and hanging in the restaurant right by the door. Mary features and sells my wines. My brochures are prominently placed by the door, next to the menus. Simply stated, the Gold Vine Grill is now a marketing tool for the Berry Factory. I'm a marketing tool for them. We're both excited to support each other.

Everybody has stuff happen to them, bad stuff and good stuff. You need to take that stuff, play with it, and see if you can use it to your advantage. You just never know what opportunities will arise, even when you least expect them.

The Unknown Future

Here we go back to that "daily bread" thing again. There's a reason I need to keep meditating on this prayer. We cannot know the future. Right now we are in a particularly nasty recession, and I don't know how it will play out—no one does. I must be ready to take advantage of whatever does happen. I may need to start again.

This was one of the lessons when I began my new company, the Berry Factory. You always have to be ready—and willing—to go back to the beginning. You may have to expand with new product lines or new ways to produce, distribute, and sell what you have. Or maybe you will have to cut back and do the things you used to do when you were just starting out. But depend upon it: conditions change, and when they do you will have to change with them.

The tough economic times we are experiencing now are a good example of this principle. My brother Rick once told me that hard times make your company stronger. You learn more during difficult times than you do when times are fun and easy. And hard times shake out some of your competition, so when the economy rebounds, as it always does, you will be in a stronger position if you have been making the right adjustments and you're still here.

Making those adjustments isn't easy; change never is. I sell a luxury product—no one actually *needs* chocolate-covered strawberries. Luxuries are usually the first things people cut back on when the economy is bad. In short, recessions make my sales go down.

Added to this challenge is that people are buying more and more online, and I had four retail stores. The Berry Factory sells online and delivers, so we don't need all that brick and mortar. I needed to consolidate, meaning I had to close one of my stores. It felt like selling one of my own arms. I couldn't hire as many temporary workers, although I managed to hang on to my core employees. But oh, it has been really, really painful.

Yet I'm also venturing out into new territories and taking new risks. I'm adding new product lines, which necessitates setup costs and learning new technologies. I hired a writer to help me write this book, another expense. With the money not flowing as easily as it was, these are leaps of faith. I'm cutting back and branching out at the same time.

Recently I purchased all my boys' names as domains. The Internet will keep growing and expanding, and who knows what the technologies will be when my boys are taking their first steps into their adult lives? So I own PaxtonFitzpatrick.com, HoganFitzpatrick.com, and MaxFitzpatrick.com. Maybe they won't need or use them—but then again, maybe they will.

The only thing I know about the future is that it is coming. When it gets here, I am going to welcome it.

A New Beginning: The Berry Factory

The most painful change I've ever gone through was the "divorce" from Shari's Berries International. Afterward I felt as though a part of me were missing. I mourned the loss for a few years, but I did recover. I picked up the pieces and moved on, developing new chocolate-dipped strawberry products, starting another online business selling gourmet gifts, and, best of all, continuing to do what I love: making beautiful, edible gifts that make people happy.

With the Berry Factory, I recovered much of what I lost when I was no longer the CEO of Shari's Berries. I am back to where I was when I started Shari's Bear'ys—out there in front of my customers. I had let myself get distanced from them when I was on the board of SBI. But now I again make sure my own pixie dust is on all our products. I go to events again, as I did years ago. I'm visible and I'm here. From the feedback I get from my customers, they like it.

There's a huge payoff here for me—I'm having fun again. New ideas are popping into my head all the time. Fruits other than strawberries, new packaging ideas, new distribution ideas—oh, my brain is bubbling away.

Right after I launched the Berry Factory, I thought we should mix it up with another fruit product. So we introduced "Clusters," red seedless grapes still on the vine, dipped in dark, milk, or white chocolate, and dusted with an edible golden powder. They were wonderful, and they went great with my Zinfandel wine, too. But as I've said, sometimes even great ideas don't work for one reason or another, maybe just timing. I loved the Clusters, but they just weren't selling, so we have pulled them for now. I still hope to reintroduce them later. Another start-over—but start-overs are good.

Then there's the development of, finally, a sugar-free product that actually tastes delicious. For years, customers have requested a sugar-free chocolate-dipped strawberry. So many people are diabetics and cannot eat my creations. I'm sad about that, but all the sugar-free chocolate coatings that I tasted were *horrible*. Every time someone requested a diabetic-friendly chocolate, I wanted to tell them that we only made stuff that tasted great, sorry, please go somewhere else. (I didn't say that, of course!)

But now a new sugar-free chocolate is out and it is truly yummy! It's a chocolate that contains Maltinol, a sugar substitute that is lower calorie and doesn't require insulin to digest it. I'm a chocolate expert, and I can hardly taste the difference between it and our regular coating. So now we do offer a great sugar-free product that I can be proud of.

In the summer of 2010, we launched our frozen line, after testing it for months. It's been an exciting learning experience and has solved one of my most difficult problems, which has been what to do with undersized strawberries. My premium fresh strawberry line can only use the large- to medium-size berries, so the small strawberries can represent a huge waste. For twenty years I bashed my head against the wall looking for ways to use them. Years ago, when I was on the board of SBI, I actually thought about freezing them and brought it up with the board. I thought we could do it on a national level, which would be a great way to use the small berries. But nobody else liked the idea, and it died.

Now it's different. I found some cute little freezers with glass doors on the front, and we initially made just enough small frozen chocolate-dipped strawberries to use up the small berry overflow, instead of giving or throwing them away. Until recently I couldn't do this on a big scale because of the huge investment in equipment, even though I had big retailers very interested and we could hardly keep them in stock.

But now we're all set to do this on a big scale nationally! The story of how it came about is in the next chapter, which is about what you can do when you don't try to do it all by yourself.

And guess what? Remember my problem with fresh cherries? Well, my new frozen line actually has an amazing frozen cherry product—without pits!

It's funny how creativity works. As soon as we figured out a way to use small strawberries by freezing them, another way showed up. We introduced what I called "Doubles." We take two smaller-sized berries and dip them together. We dip one berry and put it on the tray, then dip another one and push it into the first one. Together they form one great big berry! It almost looks like a heart. I don't know why it took me twenty years to figure this out. It keeps our costs down because we can use all the smaller berries—and besides, people think they're getting two for the price of one! The customers are happy; we're happy.

I'm not done yet. After I get the frozen line going strong, new ideas will occur to me, I know it. Maybe I'll institute a "Shari's Birthday Party" offering. If I can get our insurance company to go for it, people can rent a roped-off area of our factory to hold birthday parties. Or maybe I'll partner with an in-house party company and host "Shari parties" along with jewelry or clothing offerings. People could make their own party favors and desserts.

I'm not the only one coming up with ideas. It's kind of contagious. Take my mom, for instance. Mom is the one who named my first company Shari's Bear'ys, and she's the one who painted my lady bear logo on the wall of my first store. And now she's come up with another new "bear" idea—Teddy Bear'ys. They're chocolate-dipped strawberries that look like teddy bears: dark or light chocolate with contrasting swizzles making the teddy bear face and almonds making the ears. Those Teddy Bear'ys are so cute. And they take me right back to my roots, my mom and her bears.

A Berry Good Tip

Because radio advertising has been my most successful marketing strategy, here are three tips I've learned over the years on how to get the most bang for your radio buck. Radio might be "old" technology, but I've found that it's still the best and most economical way to get your name out there, whether you're a startup or an old hand.

One: Know the top radio stations in your area. Studies are often done on the largest radio audiences. Sometimes these results are published in local newspapers or magazines or on the Web. You want to be featured on the most successful station that you can afford, that runs promotions for products like yours. It is important that you know your demographics and market on those stations that serve your type of customer. For example, if your customers are mostly women, you probably won't get the best results on a sports station.

Naturally, the most successful stations are the most expensive and their promotion directors the hardest to get to. Don't let that discourage you. Start at the top and work your way down. Listen to the stations first to find out which of their programs run promotions or have a giveaway format if you want to do giveaways. The stations will be more interested in working with you if you're familiar with them and if they think you are a fan.

Two: Know who does what at each radio station, and develop a relationship with them. The promotion director is responsible for all promotions during programming. Most promotion departments are looking for new and fun giveaways or prizes. Why shouldn't it be your product? It pays dividends to befriend anyone in the promotion department, even if it's "just" an assistant. (Assistants often get promoted, you know.) Other relationships to develop include the DJs, who tend to be creatively involved in developing their shows and on-air personas, and the sales department—if you purchase air time, you have a better chance of working with promotions.

Three: Find a promotional tactic that works best for you. These include giveaways in exchange for product mentions, offering your product or service as contest prizes, buying recorded spots, or a combination of all three. Make sure you find the best time slots that fit your tactic and product. For instance, in most cities the morning drive time is the best slot for giveaways. Stick with one time slot for a while so you can build a relationship with the DJ and the listeners.

****

Shari's Secret Recipe #7
Clay's Banana Boats and Candied Apples

Banana Boats

1 ripe banana per person
Handful of marshmallows
Handful of Reese's™ peanut butter cups, caramels, mini candy
**   bars, or combination**

Candied Apples

1 large red apple per person
Handful of Red Hots™ or cinnamon candy pieces

For Banana Boats: Slice each banana in half lengthwise, keeping the peel on and not slicing all the way through. Stuff the banana with the marshmallows and candy. Close the banana. Wrap the banana in foil, then put in a fire pit near the hot coals. Leave in pit for 10 to 15 minutes, turning a few times to make sure the heat is evenly distributed.

For Candied Apples: Core the apple from the top, but do not core all the way to the bottom. Leave the bottom of the apple intact. Fill the empty core with Red Hots™ or cinnamon candy pieces. Wrap each apple in foil (of course—Clay loves foil!). Place wrapped apples in the coals. Leave in the coals for about 20 minutes, turning occasionally.

Chapter 8

Get Help and Use It Wisely

What do you see in your mind when you hear the word "strawberry"? Strawberries and cream, strawberry shortcake, strawberry jam, strawberry ice cream? Those are all good things, but let's mix it up a little. What else can we do with strawberries?

What about strawberry salsa? Finely chop up some strawberries, a small amount of red onion and cilantro, and kiwi. Throw in other berries if you feel like it. Let the mixture sit in the refrigerator for an hour or overnight, so the flavors combine, and then serve it with roast pork or chicken.

How about strawberry chicken salad if you have leftover chicken? Or use beef or pork—you get the idea, any leftover meat. Mix sliced strawberries with fresh greens, diced meat, and sliced almonds. Dress the salad with vinaigrette.

Do your kids like pancakes? You can mix finely chopped strawberries with pancake batter to make them even better. Believe it or not, maple syrup goes great with strawberries.

The English serve a drink they call strawberry fizz. It's simply crushed strawberries and sugar with champagne poured over it. Yum.

I have two favorite unusual ways to use strawberries. One is strawberry pizza. I already gave you the recipe in chapter 5. The chocolate crust makes it uniquely mine. But when you make it, I hereby give you permission to call it yours. I promise that your family will love it.

My other unusual strawberry favorite is a chocolate-strawberry martini. Yes, I know that martinis are usually made with an olive or onion garnish, not a strawberry, and they are supposed to be savory, not sweet. I don't care. My chocolate-strawberry martini will be the best martini you ever drink. And just to make sure you do it right, there's a recipe for it in this chapter. I must be feeling generous today.

* * * *

Jim and Janett Jacobson are my parents' friends and were our neighbors in Klamath Falls when I was in high school. By now we count them as family. Dr. Jim (he's a retired dentist) has a bah-humbug, grumpy manner that has cowed generations of children, but for some reason he took a liking to me. He thought I was a go-getter and he loved to give me advice, probably because I usually took it. It was always good advice. When my business began to succeed, I think Jim was nearly as proud as Mom and Ben.

One morning when I was visiting my parents, Jim and Janett joined us for breakfast. My business was in its sixth or seventh year at the time, and I was feeling overwhelmed because I'd been working so hard. I really needed the TLC that a trip home provided.

Jim looked at me thoughtfully. "The only thing I don't like about being a dentist," he said, "is that I always have to be there. If I'm not at work, I don't make money. You, on the other hand, are lucky. If you do it right, your business can function without you for short periods while you take a break, and you'll still be making money. In fact, that should be your ultimate goal—to structure your business and position your employees so that the business can run successfully without you having to be there."

I have never forgotten Jim's advice. Like always, it was right on the money. I had been making the same mistake many entrepreneurial women make. I didn't think I had enough money to hire people to help me, plus I believed that my personal touch had to be on every single thing I did, from scrubbing the countertops to writing every check to dipping the strawberries. Not to mention the marketing, promotions, sales, deliveries, dealing with my suppliers, negotiating contracts . . . you get the idea. I tried to do everything myself—even the things I hated to do, which of course were also the things I wasn't very good at.

Hire People Who Do Well What You Don't

Just like Ben when he wanted something, I finally made a list. I listed the things I wanted to off-load, as soon as I could afford it. And the more I thought about it, the more I realized that I could afford it sooner than I would have thought possible. For instance, I hate paperwork. My records of sales and profits were nearly non-existent during the first years of my business. I used to dream about the luxury of having my own private accountant so I never had to fill out an IRS form again. But wait—maybe I didn't have to hire a full-time accountant; I could start small, by hiring a part-time book-keeper. And that's what I did. The bookkeeper I found was the first employee I hired specifically to help me with tasks I didn't want to do, so I could spend my time doing what I was best at. She looked at my "records" and told me that I was like an ostrich with her head in the sand or a horse with blinders on. I love people who tell me the truth! She is still with my company today. (As an aside, her name is Sheri, and later on when I hired a delivery driver, her name was Sherry! *And* we all had the same middle name—Lynn. I used to joke that to come work for me it was a prerequisite to be named Shari.)

I thought I'd died and gone to heaven when I was able to hire an assistant who helped me with the rest of my paperwork—organizing my desk and files, keeping my calendar straight, stuff like that. But I *knew* I'd died and gone to heaven when I hired my second-in-command, Glenda.

One of the things I really hate to do is manage people. I know this sounds strange coming from the owner of a successful corpora-tion, but it's true. I hate conflict! I want everyone to like me, and I never want to be the bad guy. My first instinct is always to trust what someone tells me. These qualities might make me a fun person to be around, but they also make me pretty terrible at HR, especially interviewing, hiring, and firing.

Glenda came to work for SBI in 1998, at the same time I gained a partner and naively ceded control of the just-starting online division of the business. Although I didn't know it at the time, Glenda was the true gem, maybe the only gem, that I got out of that deal. When I left SBI and started the Berry Factory, Glenda came with me. I do not know how I would run my company without her. She is the chief operations officer, my right hand. She runs the company when I'm not there, and often when I am.

She is awesome at everything I'm horrible at—organization, paperwork, insurance issues, HR issues, hiring, firing, inter-viewing, reprimanding, just about everything. The only person I would ever have to fire is Glenda, and I know I'm safe because I could never do that. Everyone else works for her. She's the only one who reports directly to me. She frees me up to be the leader of the company, while she makes it run. Glenda and I make an awesome team.

Delegating is a skill that every entrepreneur must learn to do well, and it is also one of the hardest things for me to learn. But now I know that delegating frees you up to spend your time doing not only what you enjoy most but what you are good at. This is a recipe for business success. You'll make more money that way, plus you'll have more fun. You don't have to hire everyone as employees. You can contract with freelancers or contract workers, depending on what kind of tasks you are delegating. You have more control with employees, plus the employees feel more ownership, but freelance workers are great if they are doing tasks you don't need all the time. I regularly contract with writers, graphics designers, photographers, delivery firms, and especially the IT "techies" whom we couldn't live without. Everyone else I try to hire as full- or part-time employees.

The bottom line is to surround yourself with the best. You get credit for their expertise, making you look good, and their projects get completed in the most professional way possible. Even if they seem to cost more in the short term, you will get better results in the long run, and that's what it's all about.

Keep Doing What You Do Best

I want to work where it's fun. I think the Berry Factory is like Disneyland, the happiest place on earth. We push chocolate-dipped strawberries on people, and they love it. We're around yummy stuff that smells good and looks good. We play with our hands and create things that make people happy. And everyone gets to do what they love to do and do best, including me!

My fortes are product development, marketing, sales, and publicity. I'm good at these things. New ideas in these areas burst out of me like tulips in spring. I don't want to delegate here, and if I did, the company wouldn't have that "Shari" touch.

When SBI was sold, I hired a PR firm for the first time. I was concerned about possible negativity about the company being sold, so I thought they could help me with damage control if necessary. It turned out there wasn't any negativity, from the press or the shareholders, at least not any pointed in my direction. But it was nice to have the professional PR support at the time. In hindsight, however, I could have done it all myself. Mostly what they did was reinforce my ideas and provide me with reassurance that I knew what I was doing.

Whatever your forte is, whatever you love to do and do really well, keep doing it.

A Warning

Maybe the most important thing about delegating is knowing when it's appropriate and when it's not. You will need help, but be careful whom you trust. Do plenty of due diligence, and always understand who makes the final decisions. (Hint: it should be you.) Don't sell your soul or give away your power. You can have partners, but never get below 51 percent ownership if you want to retain control of your company. I learned this the hard way, and it cost me a bundle of money and more heartache than I could have imagined. I made some big mistakes in this area, which I'll talk more about in chapter 10.

There are many easy—and safe—ways to get the benefit of other people's expertise without spending a lot of money or losing control of your product or service offering. You just have to be willing to ask questions of the right people.

Picking Brains

I drive my warehouseman, Don, nuts. He'll tell me, "No, we can't do that because we don't have this"; or "No, we can't get that thing we need"; or "No, there's no way to do that." And I'll come back with, "There must be a way to get what we need. I'm not giving up." What drives him nuts is that half the time I will find that way. I'll listen to him tell me that I can't have whatever it is I want, and then a week later I'll come up to him and say, "I know you don't want to hear this, but you know those special boxes we needed? Well, I found another company who had a similar problem to us, and I called them and they told me the name of a company in Michigan who makes

just what we need. And our new boxes will be here in two days."
Don will say, "Aargh!" and then laugh.

It's another cliché—why reinvent the wheel? If you have a problem
or an unmet need, nine times out of ten you're not the only one who
has had that problem or need. Someone out there has probably already
solved your problem or met your need. You just need to find them.
This strategy has worked very well for me for years. I believe that it
is one of the primary reasons why my companies have lasted so long.

I mine my suppliers and vendors for ideas all the time. They deal
with other companies like mine, so they know useful stuff. I tell them
what I want or need and ask them if they've heard of anything similar. Have any of their other customers faced a situation like mine? If
so, what did they do? There's almost always something. Then I take
what someone has already done and adjust it to fit my own needs.
Sometimes I can even make their ideas better.

One major challenge came when we went online and national—
how to ship perishable, fragile, chocolate-dipped strawberries across
the country. I'd always been local before, so I had no idea what
packaging to use or even where to start looking for it. But I did
know who did this very thing—Harry and David, who were known
for their high quality of perishable, fragile produce shipped all over
the country. "We need to call Harry and David and talk to their head
packaging people," I told my new partner in the online business.
Later on we had trouble working together, but in the beginning he
and I made a good team. He got right on the phone and was able to
get hold of the head of packaging at Harry and David. He just asked,
"So who does all your packaging?" Sometimes it's that simple.

The guy at Harry and David didn't tell us much. After all, we were
their competition, although at that time they'd never heard of us.
But we did get a lead to a packaging consultant, who gave us a basic
blueprint that enabled us to design all the packaging and shipping
materials that we still use today.

We had fun testing our new packaging. We packed a dozen chocolate-dipped strawberries in our new package and used it as a football
in a pickup game in the warehouse. Then someone held the package
in one hand and did cartwheels from one end of the warehouse to
the other. We were like Jim Carrey as the UPS driver in the beginning of the movie *Pet Detective*, who ended up totally crushing the
package he delivered. Then we wanted to test how the packaging

would work if the product arrived on someone's porch in Dallas, Texas in July and sat there all afternoon with the sun beating down on it. But it was wintertime, so we took the package to my house and put it in the oven. The lowest temperature the oven would go was 200 degrees, so we turned the oven on and off for a couple of hours, measuring the heat with a thermostat and keeping it at about 110 degrees. When we opened the insulated package, those chocolate-dipped strawberries were perfect. They looked and tasted great; everybody said so.

As the business grew, it wasn't just new packaging that challenged us. Growth itself is a challenge for any business, especially the need for comprehensive computer systems that will keep the business running smoothly. We were a manufacturer that delivered, and our products were perishable, so we needed a system that would run everything from inventory to manufacturing to delivery to bookkeeping. I was advised that we should have something custom made just for us, but the price for hiring a consultant to design custom software was too high for me to consider. Instead I felt we just needed to see what other companies like us were using and see if it would work for us. So what kinds of companies did what we did? My first thought was pizza places—they make a food product and deliver it fresh. And my second thought was florists—they don't work with food, but their product is just as perishable, and they deliver nationwide.

Well, guess what? There was such software available. I found one originally designed for the pizza industry that would work great with just a few tweaks for our unique needs, and I also found another that had been designed for a nationwide florist. We ended up with the floral software.

The lesson is that you don't have to reinvent the low-tech wheel, or high-tech software either. Chances are whatever you need is already here, just waiting for you to find it and put it to use.

Starting to Freeze

When I was developing my frozen line, I had three big problems. One was preserving the quality of the strawberries, one was packaging, and one was distribution.

We've all seen what happens to frozen strawberries when they thaw out, right? They turn into slush. I thought that was just the way it was, until years ago when I had a conversation at an SBI board meeting with one of our big investors, another board member. Usually those board meetings were very uncomfortable for me, but this one was not. The investor's name is George Wong, and he's a pillar of the Sacramento community. He's also very thrifty (just like me!). George liked to bring berries home with him from board meetings. But it took him a long time to eat a dozen berries, and he didn't want them to go bad, because the waste bothered him. So he put them in the freezer, and whenever he wanted a berry, he'd take out just one, let it thaw for fifteen minutes or so, then eat it right away. He claimed that it tasted great.

I didn't really believe him at the time, but later I started doing research on frozen foods for the Berry Factory. There's a lot to know about frozen foods, and I didn't know any of it. I did all kinds of research, but the research that's the most fun is the hands-on kind. I bought tubs of frozen treats, such as frozen cream puffs dipped in chocolate. Cream puffs are delicate pastry, and I figured that if they could still taste good after being frozen, strawberries might have a chance too. I found out that George was right. As long as you only thawed out what you wanted to eat right away, cream puffs and strawberries both taste great after freezing.

My next problem was packaging. I visited every single market in the Sacramento area and even some in the San Francisco Bay area. I wanted to find containers that wouldn't need special machines to close them. I didn't have the money for special machines.

I worked on this problem for over a year and couldn't find the right thing. Yet I knew someone must have solved this problem somewhere. And then one day a saleswoman from a Sacramento packaging company came into our factory with a sample of their product. It had a snap-on, shrink-wrapped lid to make a tamper-evident seal. They sold it for things like caramel corn, but it was perfect for frozen foods too. I couldn't believe it—it was exactly what I'd been looking for, it was right around the corner, and they had come to me.

Once we had the right packaging, we went to work on the design. And it's so beautiful—bright and colorful with a photo of luscious chocolate-covered strawberries on the front and a photo of me on the side next to a little story about the Berry Factory. The containers help me educate my customers about where I am today and of course give them my berryfactory.com Web site. It's packaging and marketing all in one!

The third problem was distribution. I was selling to local supermarkets, so I needed an economical local distribution firm who knew about distributing frozen foods. I got online and couldn't find out anything. So I thought, "I'll go up to my grocery store and ask, 'Who delivers Dibs to you guys?'" Dibs are those popular bite-sized, chocolate-dipped ice cream snacks, about the same size as strawberries. I got hold of the assistant manager, who told me I'd have to call the store's headquarters to find out. He gave me their 800 number. I was kind of disappointed that he didn't know, but I said, "Okay," and left. As I was getting into my car, a Dreyer's Ice Cream truck pulled into the parking lot.

I grabbed a business card and a brochure and rushed over to the truck. The driver got out; I introduced myself and gave him my card. He said, "Oh yeah, I know who you are." He was one of my customers! I asked him if he thought there was a possibility that his company would be able to distribute my frozen strawberries along with their other frozen foods. He smiled and said, "Hey, maybe," and gave me the number of his boss. A week later, I met with his boss and learned more about frozen food distribution. More spaghetti against the wall—one thing always leads to another.

A Frozen Miracle

So by early 2009 I had this new frozen line prototype. The products looked great and tasted great. I'd gotten the packaging worked out. In May 2009 we launched them on the small scale we could afford: in all of our retail stores, at the state fair, and to a local upscale supermarket. They were a hit and we had a tough time keeping them in stock. Then we got nibbles from some big-time national retailers who were interested in carrying our line.

That's when I ran into a big "but." Either you're in the frozen food industry in a big way, or you're not, because the capital investment is huge. To enter into agreements with national chains, I would need to invest over $200,000 in flash-freezing equipment. Two hundred thousand dollars is a lot of money at any time, but especially for a new venture such as the Berry Factory, right in the midst of the worst recession in eighty years.

And then—a miracle! I'm not kidding.

In April of 2010 I was invited to a private tour of a new addition to a prestigious art museum. Joyce-Raley Teel invited George and Nancy Wong, and the Wongs invited Clay and me. I wasn't sure I would go, mainly because Clay was busy that day and could not accompany me. But I wanted to see George because I hadn't seen him in a long time and I wanted to tell him that I was now working on a frozen line; one that he inspired. So I went to the tour, taking my fifteen-year-old son, Hogan, with me as my escort. Hogan loves to go to events like this; he's an entrepreneur in the making.

Before we left, I made myself a "cheat sheet" that listed the topics I wanted to talk to George and Nancy about. First I wanted to assure them that I was doing well, although the split with SBI had been very difficult. Then I wanted him to know that I was moving confidently forward with my new company and experimenting with some new and exciting products, especially my frozen line. After all, George was my "frozen inspiration," since he was the first person I'd heard of who was putting chocolate-dipped strawberries in a freezer. I was going to ask him if I could send him a sample of my new frozen berries the following week.

As it turned out, I didn't have to use my cheat sheet at all. George and Nancy had brought their family with them too, including George's grown son Terry, whom I'd met before at an SBI event. Terry turned to me and said, "Well, you sure are in the paper all the time!" I responded, "Yep, you can't write soap operas this good!"

With Hogan accompanying me, the atmosphere on the tour was relaxed and low-key, as if we were just part of a family gathering. I had a hard time keeping myself from grinning. It was so obvious to me that this was an answer to a prayer. I was just along for the ride. I kept thinking of the Bible verse Job 5:9: "For he does great works too marvelous to understand. He performs miracles without number."

After the tour we all went for a traditional Chinese dim-sum brunch, sitting around a round table. Two spots were saved for Hogan and me next to Terry. As we were chatting, Terry asked what I was working on now, and when I told him about my new frozen food line his eyes lit up. Amazingly, Terry's new venture was a food distribution company. He asked me many questions about my product. The more we talked, the more excited both of us got.

The upshot was that Terry liked what he heard and proposed that he help me launch my frozen line in a very big way. When I told him I didn't have the flash-freezing equipment I'd need, he felt that one of his clients might have the capacity and the equipment that I could lease—in Sacramento, no less! Terry had lots of other ideas on how he could help as well. He grew up in the grocery store business and was just the expert I needed.

That was on a Saturday. Terry promised to e-mail me by Monday, telling me what he'd found out. Early Monday morning, sure enough, I got an e-mail from him suggesting we tour the production facility soon. That Thursday we toured the facility, which gave us more ideas. Terry is such a genius that we ended up using an even more practical solution. (It's a trade secret that I can't share—I have to keep some things to myself!) During that week he spent a lot of time investigating just what we would need, and it looked as if the Berry Factory frozen line could be in over a hundred of his gourmet stores all over California. On Saturday, Terry found the freezer unit we'd need for our initial orders.

All this happened in one week—amazing!

I'm so excited about my frozen line. Terry's help made it possible for me to go nationwide with these new products. We launched with four fruits—not just strawberries—chocolate-dipped, flash frozen, and sold in our bright tubs at grocery stores across the country.

Not only are new ideas percolating in my brain because of this new venture, old ideas have been given new life. Years ago I partnered with a Sacramento restaurant institution, Frank Fat's, to introduce a new drink sensation—the chocolate-strawberry martini. Created by me and the Frank Fat's bartending staff, we named it Shari's Chocolate-Dipped Strawberry Martini. It's made with a blend of Stoli strawberry vodka, Godiva chocolate liqueur, strawberry puree, and cream, served in a glass swirled with chocolate and rimmed with red sugar, and topped with one of my dipped strawberries.

Wow, is it a great drink. It was even voted and published as the *best martini in Sacramento Magazine*. People loved it, but there was a problem with the dipped strawberry as a garnish. Because fresh strawberries are so perishable, too many berries were going bad before they could be used. It simply wasn't profitable for Frank Fat's to make the martinis, and they had to stop carrying our wondrous creation.

But now we have our new frozen line of strawberries, which

are great! They have a long shelf life and thus no waste. So Frank Fat's and the Berry Factory have reintroduced our chocolate-strawberry martini. Ooh, it tastes so good!

When you find experts you can trust, you can create partners. They become invested in your success, just as you are invested in theirs. They share their ideas with you, and you with them. You celebrate together and help each other over the rough spots when they show up—as they always do. The bottom line is that no one does anything alone. We're all in this together.

A Berry Good Tip

I am proud of being frugal, like my Grannie and stepfather, Ben. I don't like to spend money needlessly. But there is one place I never skimp, ever. And neither should you.

Lawyers are expensive people. It kills me to pay their fees because I never feel I can afford it. What I learned the hard way is what you really can't afford is *not* to have good counsel.

I so wish now I'd had that counsel when I ceded over half of the control of Shari's Berries back in 1998. If I had, I wouldn't have done it the way I did. It was a painful lesson, but I learned. I found out later that I should have been *required* to have my own counsel, but that lesson too came too late.

By 2006, when SBI was sold to a large corporation and I parted company with them, I made sure I had effective counsel to help me dissolve our previous relationship. I had a feeling I might need it.

Boy, was I right. When I opened the Berry Factory just ten weeks after SBI was sold, my team of attorneys was still watching over me, and it's a good thing they were. Because I could no longer use the name Shari's Berries outside of my Sacramento retail stores, I formed a new company called the Berry Factory. At one point, the new owners of SBI tried to stop me from doing so. It wasn't just the name they didn't want me to have. I guess they thought they'd bought the rights to all strawberries everywhere . . . and to *Shari*. Or maybe they just thought a company with big pockets like them could easily intimidate a little hick woman from the sticks of Oregon. Or maybe they thought they could just bury me in paperwork until I went away. They had the money and the time to do it.

But because my attorneys had been involved from the beginning of the dissolution straight through the establishment of my new company, they saved the day. For a person who hates conflict of any kind, it was a nasty, horrible experience that has taken years and some pretty steep legal bills to try to resolve. However, my lawyers proved that the big company might own SBI, but they don't own me. I can market the Berry Factory on a national level. I can market my company using my own name, Shari Fitzpatrick.

My lawyers saved my new company, my good name, and probably my sanity. So here's my tip. Even though you don't think you need a lawyer now because they're too expensive, you might in the future. Establish a relationship with a top-quality firm of attorneys before that future arrives. I promise you, they are worth every penny.

* * * *

Shari's Secret Recipe #8
Shari's Chocolate-Dipped Strawberry Martini

Chocolate syrup
Red sugar
1¼ oz. strawberry vodka
½ oz. Godiva chocolate liqueur
Splash strawberry puree
Splash cream
Ice
1 chocolate-dipped strawberry, partially sliced and fanned out

Swirl chocolate syrup inside a chilled martini glass. Rim with red sugar. Shake vodka, liqueur, puree, and cream over ice and strain into the prepared martini glass. Garnish with chocolate-dipped strawberry placed elegantly on the rim.

Chapter 9

Go for the Win-Win

*Why do some foods go together? I don't know why, but they do. Choco-
late and strawberries come to mind. Here are some more: apples and
caramel, apples and cinnamon, apples and (of course) chocolate. How
about all of these taste sensations together in one bite-sized chunk?*

*Start with a big, bright-green, fresh-off-the-tree, tart-yet-sweet Gran-
ny Smith apple. Granny Smiths are one of the most popular varieties of
apple. And some Granny Smith orchards are just twenty minutes from
my home! The Apple Hill® Growers Association has been around since
the 1960s and is made up of over fifty ranches that grow pears, peaches,
and of course apples—including Granny Smiths. I'm a local girl and I
support my local community first.*

*Okay, now you have your big juicy Granny Smith in your hand, and
it's calling you to take a bite. You could eat it just the way it is, and it
would be delicious. But wait—we make it even more special.*

*First we cut up our unpeeled apples into two- to three-inch slices. We
dip the apple slices in fresh lemon juice, so the flesh doesn't turn brown.
Then we really start to have fun. We spread a thick layer of caramel on
the skin side of the apple. Who doesn't love caramel? Caramel is made by
cooking sugar, heavy cream, corn syrup, and butter together. That rich
brown color comes from a chemical reaction between the sugar and the
protein in the cream. This is the same thing that happens when you bar-
becue meats or wear tanning lotion. (I bet you didn't know that!) Why
and how this happens doesn't really matter to me. What does matter is
the chewy texture and sweet-and-toasty taste of caramel, which pairs
perfectly with a crisp, green, Granny Smith apple.*

*Now we put our apple-caramel creation on a toothpick and dip the
whole thing in white chocolate. It's one of my essential beliefs that it helps*

to dip almost anything in something that tastes as great as chocolate. Dipping seals in the freshness of the apple and the creaminess of the caramel. The slices—which we call Caramel Apple Wedgies™ because of their shape—have a ten-day shelf life. To us, used to the twenty-four- to forty-eight-hour shelf life of strawberries, this is an eternity.

Oh, I forgot. Before we package them, we dust the dipped slices with cinnamon—and pixie dust, of course.

* * * *

I have never—not in the beginning, and not now—had a big budget for marketing. But that doesn't mean I don't have big marketing ideas.

I've built my brand by hard work, enthusiasm, and consistency. For instance, I've always been a stickler for making sure my brand is on everything—Web site, brochures, business cards. I want my customers' immediate recognition. I want their mouths to water the minute they see my logo. Nothing leaves my facility without my brand name on it.

I love marketing. If I hadn't become a chocolate dipper, who knows, maybe I would have started my own PR firm. I've turned chocolate-covered strawberries into one of the nation's favorite gifts and probably *the* most popular gift to send on Valentine's Day. In 2000, I partnered with a CD producer for a special promotion. We dipped Lionel Richie CD jewel cases in chocolate before wrapping them beautifully as Valentine's Day gifts.

I promote on a local scale too. For instance, I had a meeting with Maserati of Sacramento recently. At first glance, a car dealership doesn't seem to have much in common with chocolate-dipped strawberries. But even in this down economy, they are selling lots of cars—not just Maseratis, but Jaguars and Land Rovers too. I thought, "Maserati needs to give out a box of my berries every time they sell a car." I went down and pitched the idea, and they loved it. Naturally, they can't give away a car, but they can advertise that they'll give away a box of berries to anyone who purchases one. The car dealer wins. I win. The customers win.

Of course, I'd brought the manager a bottle of chocolate-dipped wine, a box of berries, and a box of Caramel Apple Wedgies™. He said, "I feel bad that I don't have anything to give you—you brought me all these gifts."

I smiled and gestured to those beautiful cars in the showroom. I was really just kidding, but the upshot was that he'd lend me a car to drive to an event or promotion if I'd mention the car in my press release for the event. How cool is that?

But wait—how do I do all this without a huge marketing budget?

I made my network of connections pay off for me because of one simple rule, another one of those clichés I like so much. *Go for the win-win*. Like most clichés, it became a cliché because it is true.

What does going for the win-win mean? I'm talking about strategic co-branding, or following up on opportunities for cooperative and complementary marketing. It's different from a partnership, because with co-branding and co-promotion you retain ownership and control. I look for companies that have products or services that complement mine, or that have the same type of customer base that I do, or that might want to use my products as giveaways, and I find ways that we can market together. I mainly look for companies larger than mine—sometimes much larger—so I can hang on to the coattails of their marketing plans and take advantage of their bigger marketing budgets.

Using this strategy has propelled me into some unlikely places and gotten my name in front of people who otherwise would never have heard of me and my strawberries.

Reach for the Sky

My first national marketing effort was with *SkyMall* magazine, years ago. If you've ever flown, you know *SkyMall*. You might have leafed through their merchandise magazine, which you can find in those back-of-the-seat pockets in front of you. According to their Web site, *SkyMall* reaches more than 650 million air travelers a year. Wow. I knew I just had to get my berries into their magazine.

The first time I called *SkyMall* to talk about advertising in their magazine, I discovered that the smallest ad they offered, the one in the very back that's only about one-eighth of a page, cost around twenty thousand dollars. Whoa! I thanked them politely for the information and thought, "Well, there goes that idea."

But because I believe in giving in order to get, I sent them a box of berries anyway. I got a return call from one of their sales managers, who thanked me for the beautiful berries and said everyone on the management team had raved about them—they were gone in minutes. "You should be in our catalog," she said.

I explained that being in their catalog for one quarter would eat up my marketing budget for the entire year and that maybe I'd be able to advertise with them in the future when my company had grown. Then I asked, "But would you consider doing a commission deal with us? We can share the risk. I'll give you a commission for every order that we get through you, and in return you'll charge us less every month."

"Oh no, we can't do that," she said. "We've never done that. We won't do that."

Okay, that was pretty definite. But that Christmas season I was shocked because *SkyMall* chose us as their corporate gift that year! They faxed us over a long beautiful list of all their top clients and advertisers featured in their special "guest catalog." They could have given this business to one of their paying clients, but they chose us.

The Christmas packages went out, and *SkyMall* started getting phone calls—lots of phone calls—and notes and letters and then more calls. They were floored. They called me and said, "We've never seen anything like this. People are going nuts over your berries." They added, "You have to be in our catalog. We'll do that commission deal."

We were in the next *SkyMall* magazine. But we weren't in the back; we were on the cover. And when you opened the magazine, there we were again on the front-page, right-hand read. Oh yes, *SkyMall* has worked very well for us.

It never hurts to ask for the sky. You just might get it.

What's in a Name?

Besides looking for companies with big marketing budgets, I try to introduce my products to well-known people. It's another low-cost but super-effective way of getting my business name "out there."

I'm a sports fan, especially basketball. The Sacramento Kings are *my* team. The first year we had a Web site, we invested in a Kings sponsorship to help us quickly introduce our new Web site and address to our Sacramento-area audience. To show my true colors, I dyed my white chocolate purple and dipped strawberries in it—the Kings' main color is purple. In 2009, the Berry Factory was also one of the sponsors of the WNBA Sacramento Monarchs, before they were dismantled. (What a disappointment that was.) I've also given (or hand-fed) berries to players I admire, such as Ruthie Bolton, the Olympian and WNBA star who was named Female Athlete of the Year in 1991; NBA players Bobby Jackson, Mitch Richmond, and Rick Barry; and baseball stars Dave Dravecky and Steve Sax. I even hand delivered my baseball berries to a Yankees game in New York City, because Derek Jeter had ordered some of our berries. When a famous athlete says he loves a product, people tend to listen.

Other fans of the Berry Factory are in politics. I sent a box of Caramel Apple Wedgies™ to Governor Schwarzenegger, but he's not the only powerful person that I've sent my product to. California's first lady, Maria Shriver, has received berries from me and thanked me personally—she is a big supporter of women-owned businesses in California. My COO, Glenda, and I had lunch with California lieutenant governor John Garamendi a couple of years ago, during which I asked him if there was any chance I could get a state contract to fulfill government gift orders whenever they wanted to send a gesture of appreciation or goodwill. I was partly joking, of course, but I also thought it was a good idea, and again, you've got to ask if you want to receive. Nothing has come of my idea, but who knows, maybe someday.

I've also reached out to the mayor of Sacramento, Kevin Johnson. He's a former NBA all-star, so it's even more exciting to me that he is a fan of the Berry Factory. He paid me a wonderful compliment when he said I was "one of the most creative people in Sacramento." In a recent newspaper article, he was quoted as saying that I am "one of Sacramento's treasures and an inspiration to all small-business owners looking to become a world-class success." You can bet I'll do all that I can do to help him turn Sacramento into a "world class city!"

I have purposefully sought out celebrities and plied them with chocolate-dipped treats whenever I could. I take berries to every concert I go to and every large business event that I attend, especially the ones with famous speakers, just in case I might be invited backstage or meet someone who has an "in" with the celebrity. One time Willie Nelson came to town for a concert at the Sacramento River Cats stadium. Because I was a friend of the stadium's owner, I was invited to meet Willie—on his bus!—before the show and give him a box of my berries.

"Oh, I know all about these," said Willie when he saw the box. "People send them to me all the time!" That's all I needed to hear—I suggested he return the favor by ordering my berries as holiday gifts from his laptop while he was on the road. He laughed and said he would. (And he has!) I still have the photo of me and Willie taken that night. Every time I look at it I wish I'd had my hair braided like his was—that would have made a great publicity picture. I was sad when he later cut his braids off.

Over the years my berries have shown up at celebrities' weddings, home parties, concerts, and any event you can think of. My customers include people such as Liza Minnelli, Shaquille O'Neal, Halle Berry, and Muhammad Ali. My berries have been in gift bags at the Oscars and the Emmys. They have been featured on Donald Trump's "Apprentice," "The Today Show," "The Price Is Right," and "Wheel of Fortune."

Some people complain about America's "celebrity culture." But celebrity endorsements can help you sell your products and services, if those products and services provide value to them.

Real People, Real Marketing

Co-branding and co-promotions work best when you combine them with personal relationships. If you don't have a personal connection with someone who you think can be a good prospect for co-branding, make one! And never be afraid to approach the "big guys" in your industry.

Years ago, Debbi Fields of Mrs. Fields Cookies was in Sacramento doing a signing for her new cookbook at a Mrs. Fields store. Debbi Fields is one of my heroes—she too had made a huge success out of a homemade food product. I quickly made arrangements for one of my unique berry bouquets to be hand-delivered to her during the book signing. That was the beginning. Debbi Fields went crazy over the berries, leaving me a voicemail saying how excited she was about the product. She became one of my big supporters and even invited me to her home in Memphis to pick her brain.

That was a fun day. Debbi was easy to be around, hospitable and gracious, and gave me a lot of great marketing advice, as well as business advice about setting up a board of directors. (She later accepted a position with SBI as an advisor to our board of directors.) But more than any particular advice, what I remember best was that she was so encouraging. It meant a great deal to me that Debbi Fields, this woman whom I admired so much, thought my product was awesome.

After I left her house, I went on a tour of Graceland, because I've always been a big Elvis fan. How much better can one day get—Mrs. Fields' house during the day and Elvis's house in the evening!

As well as making new connections, never be afraid to use your current personal relationships in business, if you can figure out a way that you both can win. This was the case with my arrangement with Herman Rowland, CEO of the company making the famous candies known as Jelly Belly® jelly beans. I got to know Herm when he married my girlfriend Maggie, who did graphic design work for me. I have to admit that when I first met Herm, he intimidated the hell out of me. First of all, he's a big, tall guy with a deep voice. He sort of looks like a mountain man, with a personality to match. Not to mention that he's famous! He is responsible for introducing Jelly Belly® to Ronald Reagan, when Reagan was governor of California. When Reagan was elected president, Herm made a special blueberry Jelly Belly® just for the inauguration, and he supplied over three tons of red, white, and blue Jelly Bellies for the festivities. Reagan made the Jelly Belly® brand famous, and it was all due to Herm hitching a ride on his famous coattails.

Herm still intimidates me, but I look up to him, and not just because he's about a foot taller than I am. The man knows how to market and has built a creative product line, and I learn something from him every time we talk. I love the spectacular parties he gives—Herm never does anything in a small way. At the International Fancy Food Show, which is held in January in San Francisco and July in New York, Herm throws a huge party and launches some new Jelly Belly® sensation.

During the time after I left SBI and before I launched the Berry Factory, while I was "holed up" in my mountain home, ideas were incubating in my marketing brain. One of my ideas was to design a Jelly Belly® Berry, and I wondered if I could talk Herm into a co-branding arrangement. He has an entire legal department in charge of licensing the Jelly Belly® brand for things from pillows and clothing to

Jell-O, and those licenses can cost hundreds of thousands of dollars. Since the Berry Factory was brand new, I wouldn't be able to pay anything like that. I knew that if I wanted to ride on Herm's coat-tails, I was going to have to depend on our personal relationship.

My first step was to take Maggie out to lunch and tell her my idea. Did she think Herm might go for it? Maggie encouraged me to ask him. So I did.

He said, "Sure." Just like that. As a *gift*.

The Berry Factory is the only company in the world that can do a Jelly Belly® Berry. We're licensed to have the Jelly Belly® logo right on the homepage of our Web site. I even had a display of my Jelly Belly® Berries and my brochures in New York one year for the International Fancy Food Show. Our co-branding agreement gives me exposure that I could not get otherwise. Gourmet strawberries, gourmet chocolate, gourmet jelly beans—it's a marriage made in heaven.

When you work together successfully, personal relationships will naturally form. Our brands become personal to our customers too. There really is a Shari; there really is a Mrs. Fields. We are real people. We might be Elvis fans who visit Graceland, just like you.

Some relationships are just meant to be. It was meant to be that my friend happened to marry Herm Rowland. It was a blessing that I met Harry Friedman, the executive producer of "Wheel of Fortune." But it was the time and effort and goodwill that we put into these relationships that made them a lasting win-win for all of us.

The "Wheel of Fortune" opportunity began years ago when I was still in charge of marketing for SBI. I'd gotten a call from a company in Los Angeles that placed prizes on game shows. They told me they needed a prize for a new game show and asked me if we'd be willing to donate.

Now, I'm a game-show freak. I love to watch them, and my fa-vorites are "Wheel of Fortune" and "The Price Is Right." So after I agreed to donate our products as prizes on the new game show, I asked the L.A. company whether they had any contacts on either of my favorite shows. They gave me a name to call, at the department in charge of accepting prize ideas.

We called, but we didn't get far. They thought that $1,000 worth of chocolate (a year's supply) was just way too much chocolate, and they passed. However, I don't give up easily, so one of the staff of the L.A. company went to see the decision maker of the department one last time to try to convince her to try us anyway. Here's where the blessing comes in. Unbeknownst to us, that decision maker was on vacation, and the staff member had the opportunity to meet with Harry Friedman himself. As soon as Harry heard my company name, he opened his desk drawer and pulled out my brochure. He said, "These are the best things ever. I'm already a customer. Let's do this."

The next thing I knew, I was flying to Sony Studios in L.A. I went to the taping of the show and got to meet everybody backstage. I made myself popular by bringing berries for everyone. They tape a whole week in one day—three shows with one audience, then two more shows with a second audience. In between, Charlie O'Donnell comes out and entertains everyone. I had such a great time, and everyone loved my berries so much that they invited me back for more tapings. During the third taping, Charlie O'Donnell called me onstage to tell my story to the audience during his entertainment. What a great guy.

I got to know Harry Friedman pretty well too during the tapings. He always sits right up on the stage with his computer, for the taping of every show. He's the head guy but he is the nicest, most approachable person. When his daughter was to be married, she wanted our berries at her reception, so I sent them to her. She was thrilled and Harry was very grateful.

A year or so later, I went on vacation to visit my nephew Tyler, who was in the U.S. Air Force and stationed in Germany. On the way to Europe, I stopped off in New York to play in Manhattan for a few days with my girlfriend Gena. Before I left for New York, I found out that "Wheel of Fortune" was going to be taping an offsite show at Radio City Music Hall during NBA week. I called and got us passes to the show. Because Tyler is a huge basketball fan like me, I brought a basketball with me, hoping the "Wheel" people might help me get it autographed for Tyler by NBA players. Remember, it never hurts to ask!

When we got to the taping, I went backstage to say hello to Harry. I explained to him that I was on my way to see my nephew in the service, that he'd done a tour in Iraq, and that he was now in Germany. I told Harry I had this basketball and asked if he thought there was any way he could get players, big-name players, to sign it for Tyler.

Harry put his head in his hands and said, "Shari, I just got out of a meeting where I gave my staff a big lecture about no autographs from the sports stars."

"But it's for my nephew who is serving our great country," I responded. I swear I did not whine, but I might have wheedled, just a little.

Harry sighed and said, "Give me the ball. I'll see what I can do. I'll call you tomorrow."

The next day, Harry called me at my hotel. He'd talked to the NBA people and told them what was going on. They refused to use my basketball. They got an authentic, NBA basketball. They had everybody sign it and it was waiting for me to pick it up at Radio City Music Hall. I got to take it to Tyler. Today, it is still one of his most prized possessions.

Since that time, "Wheel of Fortune" and "The Price Is Right" have given away a lot of berries. But during the last years I spent at SBI and after I left, I lost touch with Harry Friedman in a personal way. The marketing department at SBI handled the relationship instead, although I don't think they thought about it in terms of a "relationship."

After the Berry Factory was up and running, one of the projects I gave myself was to work on getting back in touch with the national contacts I'd made. Without telling any sob stories or indulging in sour grapes, I wanted to tell them about my new company and the new plans I had for it.

By that time I'd lost Harry's e-mail address, so it took us some time to find him, but we finally did. It turned out that Harry had no idea that I'd left SBI. He gave me a warm "welcome back," and I sent a gift package with wine and my new Caramel Apple Wedgies™. I received a call from that L.A. company confirming that Vanna White simply loved the Wedgies.

And a month or so later, the Berry Factory was one of the prizes on the "Wheel"! I received a confirmation that they had interest in featuring some of my new products several times a year.

"Wheel of Fortune" has led to many other opportunities. People in the entertainment business know each other. They work on their relationships too.

I was featured in *Chicken Soup for the Entrepreneur's Soul*, by Jack Canfield, Mark Victor Hansen, and Dahlynn McKowen. That led to my appearance on Whoopi Goldberg's show, taped in New York. At the time, Whoopi was working on a new possible project with the Chicken Soup books publisher, and she wanted to do a show with others who had done a Chicken Soup book. Whoopi chose me and another entrepreneur who was also a contributor to *Chicken Soup for the Entrepreneur's Soul* to be on her half-hour live show. We did the show in her studio overlooking Times Square. I had a blast. Whoopi was so nice, easy to be around, and of course very funny.

People do business with people. The personal relationships you make are what support you in both good and bad times.

Win-Wins Are Everywhere

It's not only for my berry business that I look for win-wins. I look for them in my personal business too. I promise that if you look for them, you will find them. A good example in my life is real estate. My time as a mortgage broker might not have been my dream job, but it was valuable all the same. Because of my mortgage experience, I've never paid a real-estate agent for selling a house. I've always been able to trade properties.

When Clay and I got married, I moved into the house he had purchased some time before, moving out of my tiny condo. In the new house, I fixed up a room for my office and did business there until I could get my first location. Although bigger than my condo (that wouldn't be hard), the house was fairly small, only 1,100 square feet. We began our family, and the house seemed to get progressively smaller as first Paxton and then Hogan arrived. By then it was wall-to-wall furniture, cribs, and toys. When you went outside, though, it was beautiful—we'd worked hard to improve the property. After all, Clay is in the building trade. To say he is handy is a big understatement.

We wanted to move, but the market was upside down. We put so much into the property that we owed about the same that the house was worth. We had watched a new forty-house subdivision get built across the street from us, full of lovely homes. (Although when they first cut the trees down to start building, we signed a petition trying to stop them, which wasn't successful. Now I'm glad it wasn't.)

One day Clay and I rode our bikes through the subdivision to look at the houses. Most of them were sold; in fact, there was only one left, in the back of the development. The minute I saw it I knew it was perfect for us. I went home and started thinking about how we could possibly get out of our current home and buy that perfect house.

I called the property owners, Elliott Homes, and simply asked,

"Do you ever consider trading homes?" They said, "Yes, we do that sometimes. Harry Elliott himself goes out about once a month to look at properties to possibly trade." They told me he was coming in just a few days, so I gave them my name and address and asked for him to come and see me.

A few days later, Harry Elliott and one of his staff showed up at my house. Rain was driving in sideways from a black sky that day. It felt like a typhoon. But just when I opened the door to Harry, the rain stopped and a blue circle of sky appeared right above my house. I'm not kidding. The sun shone through the clouds and made everything bright and beautiful. The wet grass glistened, and my house, of course, was perfectly clean—I'd spent hours making sure of it. (And with two little boys underfoot, that is something to brag about!)

Harry looked around at the crowded rooms and said, "I can see why you need to move." He told me that he had one house left, and he really wanted to close that subdivision up. Until all the houses were sold, he had to have a staff working there. In other words, he was as motivated as I was. We put the deal together. I even got him to give me more money than my house was worth and to give me a great deal on the new house. I did my own loan through my brother's mortgage firm, so I didn't have to pay any points. Elliott Homes sold all the homes in the development and no longer had to staff it. We both won.

We lived in that house about eight years, until it was paid off. By that time, I was ready to move again. I was going through the heartache with SBI and wanted nothing so much as a peaceful place to lick my wounds. Our house was no longer that place. The boys, who now included Max, were bigger and noisier with lots of friends. We were close to a busy street with a lot of street noise, and our next-door neighbors were just that—right next door. You could literally jump from roof to roof. I started to feel claustrophobic. "I've got to get out of here" was the sentence that kept going through my head.

It wasn't just for me, either. I wanted to move my boys to a place with more room, not only inside the house but outside. They were watching too much TV and eating too much McDonald's. I wanted them to play outside, get dirty, and grow up in the country, the way Clay and I did in Oregon.

I got out my famous yellow pad and made another list. I listed all the things my perfect home would have, starting with where it would be. I wanted to move to the foothills, up in the pine trees near the heart of the Fair Play wine country. It was one of our favorite camping areas, so I was familiar with its beauty.

Writing your dreams down is a powerful way of making them come true. It wasn't long before I got an online lead on a family who owned five acres and a big house in the Fair Play region. They'd actually owned the property for ten years but just recently built the house; in fact, the house wasn't quite finished. They designed it as their dream home, but when they moved up there, the wife and two teenage daughters found out they didn't like living so far away from Sacramento and all their friends.

I sent this family a box of berries and a note that took me three weeks to write, saying, "Let's trade houses. I understand you want to move to Sacramento." It turned out that the wife's sister had just moved to a new home—under a mile away from where we lived! Our house was perfect for them.

Their home was perfect for us too. It has everything I wrote on my list. It's only nine miles from the lake. We have tangles of wild blackberry bushes and a little pond on the property. I have a big office at home. My job, besides managing the financial stuff, is product development and marketing. Although my house is far away from my retail stores and factory, today's technology makes it possible for me to do a lot of my work at home. I can be at home with my boys much of the time and savor their growing-up years. The boys can get as dirty as they want. They can play ball outside without the danger of breaking someone's window. They can shoot and fish to their hearts' content. The beauty of the countryside makes all of us thankful for God's amazing bounty.

There's often a way to get what you want if you can find a way to get someone else what they want. This really does work.

Winning with Wine

One of my biggest successes in co-branding has been my entry into the wine market. I got the idea to dip wine bottles in chocolate when I was in my first retail store, when a bride-to-be asked if there was a way we could dip the champagne bottles in chocolate for her wedding reception. I thought that was pretty creative, especially the embedded pull-string we designed to get the chocolate off the bottle.

Over the years we have chocolate-dipped a variety of California wines. The first "wine person" I met in my new neighborhood was winemaker Michael Beem, who worked for Toogood Winery then. Michael and I became good friends. He's passionate about wine-making and knows simply everything about it. Listening to him talk about his wines is almost as good as drinking them.

Michael kept telling me that I needed to do my own wine. He wanted to help me develop it. I knew it was a great idea, but things at SBI were going from bad to worse at that time, so I told him that I had an idea percolating and hopefully I'd be able to do it later.

My love for the area grew as I got acquainted with the winemakers there. My taste for and knowledge of wine grew too. In fact, I'd say I developed into a "wine snob." I now know the difference between the best wines, the good wines, and the so-so wines. I can tell instantly if a bottle was opened a day before, and I won't drink it. In short, I only drink the best.

So when I started the Berry Factory, doing my own wine was close to the top of my to-do list. (Yes, of course I made another list!) By that time, Michael had moved to a different winery called Perry Creek. Perry Creek is the largest producer in this area, and they just happened to have a new owner. It was a good time for me to go in and pitch my idea to him, with Michael's help, of course. He told Perry Creek, "If you let me make Shari's wine here, she'll be marketing for you, right here where it's made." The winery would be listed on the back of every bottle of wine sold through the Berry Factory. It would be my coattails that would be ridden on this time. It would be a win for them.

For me, I saw the wine as a great way to market not only the product itself but the Berry Factory name. It was another way for me to tell my story and educate people that the Berry Factory was a new brand that I was heading up and it had a different Web site address.

Perry Creek went for it wholeheartedly. They let me have full access to their entire inventory of wine in the barrel. They let me use their estate Zinfandel, which was grown right on the property. The reason we chose a Zinfandel is that I live in a Zinfandel appellation; in fact, this area is one of the earliest sites of Zinfandel plantings in America. The soil and the microclimate here are perfect for growing Zinfandel grapes.

At first, we were going to blend my favorite Zinfandel. I like a really dry wine with a lot of tannin. But the more I researched people's tastes, the more I realized that my taste was too dry for many people. I didn't want to limit my customer base, so we blended something more middle of the road. Michael added 10 percent Petite Sirah to the Zinfandel. Michael is the most passionate guy about wine I've ever met. He grew up in wine country, and it's in his blood. I trusted his expertise.

I also learned to trust Clay's palate, which is funny because Clay had mostly been a beer guy, not a wine guy at all. Before we moved to the wine country, his main experience with drinking wine was a sweet White Zinfandel that would make him gag today. But he learned fast, and it turned out his palate was perfect for selecting a wine that most people would love. We tasted and tasted, and I brought up more people to taste our blends—white wine drinkers, red wine drinkers, beer drinkers, you name it. But I knew it was the right blend when Clay said, "This is it. This is the blend." Michael agreed, and the first Shari's Grand Reserve was born: Sierra Foothills Zinfandel 2005.

I designed my own labels (with my signature *S*) and did my own corks. I hired Perry Creek to do the bottling and store it for me. We made it available chocolate-dipped and undipped and sold it through BerryFactory.com and my four retail stores in Sacramento. We've done four bottlings so far.

It's an amazing wine. I love the way wine is described, don't you? The description of ours went something like "demure yet robust with a bouquet of vanilla and coffee and the flavors of black cherry and spice." We entered the wine in the 2006 El Dorado fair, the first time I entered a bottle of wine anywhere, and it won Double Gold! I don't know if it gets any better than that.

The Zinfandel is just the first of many Shari's Grand Reserve wines. Michael introduced me to his friend John Miller of Miller Vineyards (MV), a world-renowned winemaker. His Syrah won the 2009 award for Best Syrah in the Pacific Rim, a huge honor. As soon as I met John I tried to talk him into doing a wine with me, but he refused because he had limited inventory. But then the grower for his Syrah grapes offered him a great deal if he'd buy double the amount he usually bought. When I heard this, I told him, "The whole reason this happened was so that you could do a wine with me!" He laughed and agreed, and now my next Grand Reserve will be a Syrah made by John! How exciting is that?

And now I look forward to making a Zinfandel Port together with Michael at his new winery, Garnet Sun. It's something else that he's encouraging me to do! Well, he was right the first time, and I expect he will be right again.

Who knew that chocolate-dipped strawberries would lead me to winemaking? My relationships with the winemakers in my community have blessed me richly not only in business but in friendship.

Right across from Michael's tasting room is a gorgeous golf course called Apple Mountain. Clay is big on golf and so are my sons. While the boys are playing a round or hitting balls at the driving range, I often go across the street and help Michael in his tasting room if he's busy, which he always is—shoulder to shoulder and wall to wall with people. People love to be around Michael. He's like a big teddy bear, all friendly and welcoming.

Not too long ago, I walked in and saw the usual crowd of people. "What do you want me to do?" I asked, and he said, "Start pouring." I poured for a while, and then he had to leave to get more wine from the cellar. I poured faster. Then I saw we were running out of glasses. When Michael came back with more wine, I started washing glasses. He kept pouring and I kept washing glasses for a good hour.

My brochures are on Michael's counter, and one of the guests picked one up to read about my chocolate strawberries. "These look good," he said to Michael, and Michael answered, "Yes they are, and that's Shari right back there!" He pointed at me, up to my elbows in soapy water. I just turned my head and said, "Hi. I got a promotion. I'm now a dishwasher."

When John Miller won the Best Syrah in the Pacific Rim award, seven dignitaries from Anaheim came to hand-deliver the award. John's tasting room wasn't ready yet. He and his wife, Cindy, were scrambling to get it together before the dignitaries arrived. My mom and her talented girlfriend happened to be in town, and I took them by to see John's new tasting room. We got there just as the UPS truck pulled up and delivered boxes and boxes of stuff needed for the displays and the retail sales room. We saw that John and Cindy needed help, so we pitched in. We got a hammer and ladder and went to work putting up the displays. I ran to my home "stash" and brought back a bunch of chocolate strawberries for him to serve with his wine and impress those dignitaries no end.

One of the paintings I hung up was a triptych, a three-panel painting, of a dazzling saloon girl all in red and black. Those are the colors in the décor of my retail stores, and I just fell in love with that painting. After the dignitaries left, John gave it to me, although he asked if he could keep it in his tasting room because it is such a conversation piece. When people inquire about it, as they often do, he tells them whom it belongs to and hands them one of my brochures.

Community and co-branding go together naturally, as do co-branding and friendship. One feeds the other, and we all win.

A Berry Good Tip

In 1990, when Shari's Bear'ys was only a year old and before I had my first retail store, Nordstrom opened its first store in the Sacramento area. I love Nordstrom, always have, and I was excited that I wouldn't have to go all the way to San Francisco to shop there. There was another reason for my excitement too—Nordstrom has a gourmet food section. It was obvious to me that they should carry my berries!

Well, why not? So what if they were a huge successful corporation and I was a little startup working out of my apartment all by myself? I knew my berries were a perfect fit. The only reason Nordstrom didn't know it was because they hadn't heard of me yet.

So I placed a phone call to Jim Nordstrom. I was told he wasn't available, and would I like to leave a message? I said no, I'd call back. I called back and was told the same thing. I called back again. I was asked if I'd like to talk to an assistant, but I said no, I needed to talk directly to Mr. Nordstrom.

After a few more rounds of this, I stated, "I have a perishable delivery for Mr. Nordstrom. When would be a good time to get it to him?"

It wasn't a lie. I did have a delivery for him. One of my mantras is *It's better to ask for forgiveness than permission.* I don't like rules, and I break them all the time. Half the time I get in trouble, but the half that I don't is usually worth it.

The Nordstrom staff gave me a time that he'd be in the office. I showed up at that time, carrying my box of chocolate-dipped berries in its beautiful packaging. The receptionist told me I should leave it with her and she'd make sure Mr. Nordstrom got it. I politely said, "No, that's all right. I have all day, and I'll wait."

I waited for over two hours. Periodically the staff would try to persuade me to leave the delivery with them, saying Mr. Nordstrom still wasn't available. But I smiled and refused, telling them I was fine sitting there, and I'd wait until he had time to see me.

Finally I was shown into Jim Nordstrom's office. I said, "Congratulations on your new location. I'd love to have my berries in your store." And I opened up the package to show the berries in all their glory.

Jim Nordstrom loved how I got in to see him. He wasn't mad. He tried a strawberry and loved it too. He set me up with his staff, and within a few weeks my berries were in the dessert display in the Nordstrom café in the mall.

The point of this story is this: always go to the decision maker. Don't waste your time going to the people who don't have the power to say yes. They will always say no. Just go straight to the top. If you get a yes, it's a done deal. Even if you get a no, you will have saved yourself the time and energy of banging your head against a brick wall.

Be bold and ask. Most of the time, you will get what you ask for, if you've asked the right person.

****

Shari's Secret Recipe #9
Shari's Cherry and Strawberry Zinfandel Trifle

Trifle

1½ cups dry Red Zinfandel wine (Shari's Grand Reserve!)
⅓ cup sugar
1 tsp. vanilla
2 cups sliced strawberries
2 cups pitted, sliced fresh cherries*
1 box vanilla pudding
3 cups milk
1 lb. pound cake (I use Entenmann's All Butter Loaf Cake)
A few whole strawberries and cherries for garnish

Whipped Cream

1 pt. heavy whipping cream
¼ cup sugar
2 tsp. vanilla

For Trifle: In a 3- or 4-qt. pan over high heat, bring wine and sugar to boil. Boil until reduced to 1 cup, about 5 minutes. Remove from heat. Stir in vanilla and sliced strawberries and cherries. Let cool about 1 hour, stirring occasionally.

Make vanilla pudding according to package instructions, using the milk. Refrigerate.

For Whipped Cream: Use a *metal* bowl! Chill bowl and beater in fridge before you whip the cream. Whip cream with electric beater until thickened, then slowly add the sugar and vanilla. Beat until soft-peak stage. Note: Don't overwhip the cream, which will make it curdle. Refrigerate.

To assemble: Cut cake into 1½ x 2-inch chunks. To do this, cut cake into ½-inch slices, and then cut each slice in half. Arrange ⅓ of the cake chunks in the bottom of a beautiful glass bowl. Spoon ⅓ of the sliced strawberries, cherries, and wine over the top. Spread ⅓ of the whipped cream over the berries. Spread ⅓ of the vanilla pudding over the whipped cream. Repeat layers 2 more times, ending with the pudding. Cover the trifle loosely and chill at least 2 hours or up to 1 day.

Before serving, artistically garnish top layer with the whole berries and cherries. Makes 12 servings.

Tip: For true decadence, serve the rest of the bottle of Zinfandel with this dessert.

*If cherries aren't in season, you can double the amount of strawberries or substitute fresh raspberries, blueberries, or red seedless grapes.

Chapter 10

Eat Your Mistakes—They're Good for You

Let's pretend you have a box of a dozen of my famous chocolate-dipped strawberries in front of you right now. Four berries are dipped in dark chocolate, four in milk chocolate, and four in white chocolate. On top of the chocolate dip are designs made with swirls of a contrasting-colored chocolate. We call those swirls "swizzles" and the berries designed this way "swizzle berries."

Swizzles are like fingerprints we paint on the strawberries. They are unique, individual, no two exactly alike. Some swizzles are spirals; some are whorls. Some are thick, fat lines; others are delicately slender, faint as kitten whiskers. Some curve, some wiggle, and some bulge.

We're so proud of our beautiful swizzles that we created a company mascot that we take to tradeshows and fairs. Her name is Miss Swizzle. She was made by the same company who made the Jelly Belly Companies' mascots. You blow her up kind of like a hot-air balloon, and a person gets inside her. There's a fan inside, sucking air from the outside and recycling it through tiny vents, so the person stays nice and cool. And there she is, our Miss Swizzle walking around the fair or hanging out at a Sacramento Kings game, a giant chocolate-dipped strawberry with our signature swizzle design. Her name is printed across her strawberry butt.

When I first designed my berries, I was experimenting with the chocolate, trying to make them more special than just regular chocolate-dipped strawberries. That's when I accidently drizzled lines of white chocolate over the top of a freshly dipped dark-chocolate-dipped berry. Only I didn't call it a "drizzle." You know how I mix up words sometimes? Well, I meant "drizzle" but I said "swizzle." It was a mistake.

For years nobody corrected me, because they thought I was just being creative. And they were right; I was. Sometimes it's hard to tell the difference between making a mistake and being creative. Sometimes there is no difference at all.

Swizzles are like that. They're one of my best mistakes.

* * * *

I once read that if everyone stood in a circle and threw all their problems into a pile, after seeing everyone else's problems we'd quickly grab ours back. No matter how big or bad our problems seem, there are always people with bigger and badder ones. Plus, they're *our* problems. I think it's the same with mistakes. We all make them, but our own become dear to us because they are always our biggest teachers and become a part of who we are.

Another thing I once read: research done on successful people found that many had their largest success right after their largest failure. This shows that if you have the energy and tenacity to get up one more time than you get knocked down, eventually success will be yours.

Sometimes we are knocked down by others, but more often than not we are knocked down harder by the mistakes we make ourselves.

My biggest mistakes in business were made between 1998 and 2006, when I lost control of the brand I had founded in 1989. One interesting thing I found was that many of the mistakes I made then were the same kinds of mistakes I've made in other areas of my life. Other people in my stories made mistakes too, and there's blame enough to go around. But I'd rather look at my own mistakes, so I can learn from them. I can't change anyone's behavior but my own.

I'm not going to go into detail about what happened and who did what to whom, when they did it, or why. First I'll give you a short summary of "just the facts" without any useless finger-pointing, and then I'll discuss the mistakes I made and what they taught me.

Just the Facts, Ma'am

In 1998, like everyone else, I saw the potential of the Internet. In addition to my retail stores and Sacramento-area delivery business, I formed an online company, Strawberry Enterprises (doing business as Shari's Berries), and took on a partner to help me. To raise capital, we acquired investors also eager to jump on the Internet bandwagon and formed the required board of directors. Because the investors were interested in the Internet business only, my ongoing retail/ delivery business remained a separate entity from Strawberry Enterprises. I continued to have the rights to all sales in the Sacramento region, including Internet sales delivered within my area. My partner and I, and the investors, owned Strawberry Enterprises.

I was given the title of CEO, but acquiring capital, shareholders, and debt was new to me. I knew how to build a company out of profit, slow and steady; but the thought of spending money to make money was foreign. Initially it appeared we were on the right path, but as time passed and debt grew, I felt isolated because of my more conservative approach to business. I never imagined that I wouldn't always be a part of Strawberry Enterprises, and it was during this period that I gave the mark I owned, Shari's Berries, to Strawberry Enterprises. We hired a management team, including a new CEO, who changed Strawberry Enterprises' name to Shari's Berries International (SBI) and decided that I, the namesake of the company, shouldn't be allowed to represent the company. Ultimately I felt I no longer had a hand in the direction of SBI. It was a difficult time for me, but I stifled my frustration and directed my creative energy toward my Sacramento-area retail stores.

In 2005, most shareholders and I were blindsided by an attempt by management to acquire SBI. That attempt failed but in 2006 was followed by a successful acquisition by a large corporation based in San Diego. I still had my retail stores and a license to use the name Shari's Berries in the Sacramento area, but everything else was gone.

Despite the pain I felt, I moved forward and in 2006 founded a new company, the Berry Factory. My Sacramento regional business continued to operate as Shari's Berries until February 2010, when I decided to combine all of my retail operations under the Berry Factory umbrella.

That is the nutshell version. Now let's look at those mistakes I made. There were plenty. Maybe others can learn from them too.

Learning Too Late

My products had been so well received that I just knew they would be equally successful on a national level, and I would not be limited to selling in Sacramento. But in 1998 I knew little about the Internet (or technology of any kind) except I could see that the possibilities were huge. We didn't even have a computer system at the time!

So when I met a young corporate attorney who said he understood both technology and marketing on a national level, *and* he wanted to leave his law firm and go into business with me, I was thrilled. This would mean I wouldn't have to learn about technology or how to launch an Internet campaign. And since my partner would be a lawyer, I wouldn't have to spend the money to get my own attorney to educate me on setting up a partnership.

Because I trusted my soon-to-be partner, I didn't get my own counsel. I am sure my former business partner was looking out for his best interest, but I was too naive to know that I should have had someone looking out for mine. I was totally confident of my new partner's ability and jumped feet first into a business relationship that I felt would earn us both lots of money.

My mistake was that I wanted to have the fun part only. I didn't want to take the time and do the hard work of educating myself. I didn't want to be a techie, and I was proud of being a little "hillbilly girl." I had never taken a business class, yet look how successful I had become anyway! I thought my "street smarts" and hard work would pull me through, because they always had before.

But this time they weren't enough. The lesson: if you don't know something, don't risk your time, energy, and money until you learn.

Misplaced Trust

My mom once ran a small business but never a large one. She was, and is, a great homemaker, but how much could she really know about business, right? So if she gave me business advice, I felt free to ignore it. Talk about mistakes! If I had listened to my mother, the whole SBI mess could have been avoided. She advised me to run a credit report on my potential partner—on a private call she insisted on having with him! I was mortified. He was so insulted that later he told me he almost canceled doing the deal. Whether running a credit report would have told me anything wasn't really the point my mom was trying to make. She was telling me that I didn't know enough about my soon-to-be business partner. I hadn't done enough due diligence.

My business was booming, but keeping it booming was getting harder. We didn't have a single computer. I had no technical experience, and lack of technology hampered us—we just couldn't handle any more. We needed some systems. I was pregnant with my third son, Max, and so very tired, with way too much to do. To get ready for Valentine's Day 1998, I worked thirty-six hours straight, even though I knew I shouldn't. When someone promised to save me, relief blossomed into belief.

It wasn't that my partner was a bad guy. His heart was in the right place. I wanted so much to trust him, so I did. Without my own attorney to help me negotiate the business arrangement, I naively handed over too large of a percentage, one that would set me up to lose majority control of the Shari's Berries brand. At this point, my new partner now had total control over all the business decisions. He could have even fired me if he wanted to, and I would have had no recourse. At the time, I did not understand this completely. I thought we were sharing the business, and that was fine with me. I wanted to concentrate on the fun things that I loved to do—product development, marketing, and PR. He could deal with the money issues, such as recruiting investors and setting up the board of directors, and especially the technological issues that would allow us to create big sales via the Internet.

I have always been way too trusting. I like to think of myself as an optimist, but maybe I take optimism a little too far. Maybe a better word for what I am, or used to be, is gullible. I want to believe that everyone tells the truth and will do what they say they'll do. My first instinct is to believe whatever anyone tells me.

My willingness to trust people has cost me some grief with my own employees. I trust them to do their jobs, without me having to oversee every little thing they do. Sometimes this works, but sometimes it doesn't—sometimes I'm seen as a poor communicator because I just assume that people are doing their jobs the way they're supposed to be done. I don't like to be told what to do so I assume others don't either.

An example is when I had the bright idea to dip a bottle of cheap aftershave in chocolate and sell it as a promotion for Father's Day. What a dumb idea! But none of my employees told me it was a dumb idea, even though nearly all of them knew it was way before I did.

I had trusted people to tell me their opinions and save me from my own mistakes.

I've learned now that I have to examine the things I'm told before I believe them. I can't believe the first thing I hear; I have to see both sides of the story before I get all fired up.

I've learned that I need to call my own shots. Having partners can be a great thing, but never, ever, allow yourself to enter into an agreement where it would be possible for you to lose majority control of your own operation. Fifty-one percent—that's the number to keep in the forefront of your mind always. Never allow your ownership to go below it.

Being Liked Is Nice but . . .

Let me say it again: I hate conflict. I want to be liked, by everyone, always. I am really uncomfortable with any kind of conflict. This has been true my whole life.

When Clay and I were first dating, when I was a senior in high school, I made a couple of attempts to cook for him. As young as I was, I knew the truth of the cliché, "the way to a man's heart is through his stomach." One day he mentioned that he really liked stew, so I found a recipe that sounded good, and the next time I went to his house I made it for him and his roommate.

Unfortunately I didn't follow the recipe very well, only putting in about half the liquid it called for. When I took the lid off the pot of "stew" it looked more like Salisbury steak, as there was absolutely no liquid remaining—it was just meat and vegetables. It smelled great but Clay took one look and said, "That's *stew?*" in a grossed-out voice.

I was crushed. Although I tried to laugh it off, when I left I cried all the way home. He hated my stew! I knew I had ruined our relationship for all time. (I'm so glad I'm not seventeen anymore.)

Years later, when Clay and I started dating again, every other weekend he would come from Sacramento to visit me in Reno. I was determined that our relationship would work this time, so I always prepared a nice dinner for him, to be all ready when he arrived Friday night.

On his first visit, I made him Chinese paper-wrapped chicken and my mom's special fried rice. He went crazy over it, saying again and again how great it was. I felt as though I'd won the lottery. So I continued to "surprise" him with this same meal every time he visited. On his fifth or sixth visit, when I proudly set the dish before him, he said, "Huh? Paper-wrapped chicken and fried rice *again?*"

His disappointment was another crushing blow. I vowed to myself never to make that dish again. That too was a mistake. About fifteen years later, Clay asked me, "Hey, why don't you make that paper-wrapped chicken anymore? I loved that stuff!"

The lesson that paper-wrapped chicken finally taught me was that it's not a good idea to base decisions simply on whether I'll be liked or not. Someone can still like me even if we have a conflict. Clay does.

Know When to Fight

Conflicts are not always as easy to resolve as paper-wrapped chicken. Sometimes, to get through them, you may be asked to stand up and fight. I was, and it scared me to death.

When the board at SBI asked me to step down as CEO, I had little choice, due to my mishandling of the original agreement with my partner. At the time, SBI was having some difficulty in keeping the money flowing in, and the board wanted a CEO who would address that head on.

The new CEO and the board of directors had a much different vision for the company than I did. My vision was all about creative products and frugal marketing. Of course I wanted to make money, but I believed we could make money without spending on avenues that I didn't believe would help the company. The new CEO was an accountant and didn't like that we didn't have much debt. Whoops, that was a major clash! He worked hard to convince me that more debt could be healthy for the company. But when the company ended up with the new debt, the Internet bubble burst. The timing was bad.

In my view, the new CEO's vision devalued our brand—my brand, the brand I'd worked so hard and so long to build—by cheapening the packaging. He eliminated the cellophane-wrapped layers and removed the colorful holiday accents and replaced them with a plain "all-year-round" look, all to save a few pennies a box. I felt that he was messing with my artistic creation and it tore me up. He tried to take the magic away. I wanted my pixie dust, but he didn't see the value of pixie dust. To him, it was an unnecessary and expensive extra.

Yes, I expressed my opinion, but I wasn't listened to. I no longer had the authority to direct the company, and they didn't have to listen to me.

I let myself be silenced. I don't like to throw my weight around. Now I wish I had fought harder. I wouldn't have won all the battles, but I might have won some.

Besides, in the end I had to fight anyway. When SBI was sold in 2006 and I separated from the company totally, I had to stand up and fight for the right to my own name and my own ideas. It was a long, drawn-out process, and at various times I cried, threw up, or stood on shaking knees. But with the help of my lawyers, employees, friends, family, customers, and Jesus who fought with me, I did not give up.

I still don't like to fight. I want everything to go smoothly, and if it doesn't, I want someone else to fight for me. The difference is that now I know this is not always possible.

I learned to trust myself and God first. I have to be willing to fight for my vision for my products and my company. It can't be all about the money. First it needs to be about the products and the customers who love them.

Follow Your Own Advice

From around 2000 until I left SBI for good in 2006, my work stopped being fun, although I still got satisfaction from running my four retail stores and local delivery service. But working with SBI was horrible. I hated my job. I dreaded leaving my peaceful mountain home to go into the SBI office. I was miserable.

Ironically, it was during this time that I became a "poster child" for women entrepreneurs. I was widely known in Sacramento as the Strawberry Girl; they had watched me grow from my little apartment and one-woman delivery service to a nationally recognized leader in the gourmet-food industry. I was recruited onto the speakers' track and encouraged to tell my story about how wonderful it was to be an entrepreneur.

I spoke at business functions and college campuses, and my speeches nearly always began with the same piece of advice—the same one that begins this book: do what you love. But was I still following my own advice? I was not.

The more I spoke to people eager to hear how I "did it," the more I realized that I had to start over and do what I love once again. I thought I was speaking to those college kids and wannabe entrepreneurs. But really I was speaking to myself, and what I was saying was, "Follow your own advice."

Know When to Let Go

I am grateful that I kept my four retail stores and retained area and did not merge them with SBI. The painful conflict with the company that bought SBI resulted in my belief that, to move forward, I had to let go of the past.

Finally, in 2010, I renamed my stores the Berry Factory, although I still had rights to the Shari's Berries brand in my retained area. Why had I been resistant to changing the name of my stores for so long? In a word: pride.

And I don't mean pride in a good way. I couldn't give up what I'd built. I didn't want to admit I had to let go of marketing Shari's Berries. What a mistake this was. But one day, a profound thought occurred to me while I was praying: I needed to let go of Shari's Berries in order to find Shari again.

After I took the plunge and converted the stores to the Berry Factory, I've seen the difference it makes to my customers. They are more educated on the difference between the two brands. My employees are just as proud—prouder—of the Berry Factory. Now I wonder, "Gosh, why didn't I do this sooner?"

Holding on to the past is not a good idea. We all have to learn when it's time to let go.

Pruning

I've learned that God is more interested in my character than my comfort. I'm being pruned. It's like refining gold; to make it beautiful, you have to burn it. The experience with SBI was painful, but in the end it was worth it.

God allows us to suffer so that we can become better comforters. Years from now, I might be able to advise somebody else if they get in a business mess. Life is a series of lessons, one after the other, and many of them are hard. With God's help, I have come through difficult times to achieve success, and it may comfort others to know it can be done. As it says in Isaiah 30:21, "Whether you turn right or left, your ears will hear a voice behind you, saying, 'This is the way; walk in it.'"

Starting over was not easy. I had to go back to the beginning, and my pride suffered a little. But I am already recovered and moving on. I have a new business, and I am again doing what I love—creating awesome new products that make people happy. Energy sings through me. I am back to my entrepreneurial roots. I'm involved in every detail of the Berry Factory. I had become too distant from the day-to-day operations, and my customers missed seeing me. But now I communicate with my customers every chance I get. The "real Shari" is back and so is the pixie dust.

The Berry Factory will be even better than my original company, because of what I have learned. I gained so much more than I lost. We learn the most when we're down in the trenches. I can truly say that I am thankful for the whole experience, the bad as well as the good.

I'm keeping a journal, as well as memorizing Scripture and meditating on it. Now when the next hard time comes, I will be able to remind myself that mistakes are not bad if you learn from them. And good times will come again.

A Berry Good Tip

At every painful stage of my life, during the time I was living it, I thought that *this* was the hardest ever. I should have kept a journal earlier, so I could have read about past hard times and been reminded that they end. I also might have been reminded of how I dealt with them.

When Clay decided to break up with me, back when I was in college, I thought my heart was broken and would never heal again. I was sure I'd never been in such pain before. I wasn't angry; he was a great guy, and he didn't mean to hurt me—he just had his wild oats to sow. But I loved him so much, and I knew I needed to get away and start over, or the pain would overwhelm me.

So I moved away and began a life in a new location with a new job.

It worked. I still loved Clay, but I recovered my optimism and happiness. It was all a matter of gaining a different perspective.

I did the same thing when I moved to the wine country, up in the foothills away from downtown Sacramento, during the darkest days with SBI. I was exhausted, upset, angry, frustrated, and full of grief. I needed to remove myself from the negative energies swirling around me at my workplace.

But in my new foothills home, in the Sunbelt right above the fog line and right below the snow line, serenity slowly came back to me. I worked from home as much as I could. I prayed a lot. I accepted this hardship and meditated on the truth that God has a plan for me and my life. I accepted the lessons God planned to teach me.

I learned that it is okay to take a break once in a while. I don't have to be so driven all the time. I spent lots of extra time with my boys. I prayed and searched inside myself for strength, understanding, and courage, and I relied 110 percent on God's grace.

During difficult times, it helps to get off the merry-go-round and take a look at your life from the outside. Stop, really stop, for a part of every day. Take a moment to focus and meditate on what is really important. Get a new perspective.

****

Shari's Secret Recipe #10
Shari's Paper-Wrapped Chicken and Mom's Special Fried Rice

Marinade

3 tbsp. soy sauce
3 tbsp. oyster sauce
3 tbsp. hoisin sauce
1 slice fresh ginger, shredded, or ½ tsp. ground ginger
1 tbsp. sesame oil
1 tbsp. dry Shari (oops . . . I mean sherry)
¼ tsp. garlic powder
¼ tsp. onion powder
1 tbsp. sugar
½ tsp. five-spice powder

Paper-Wrapped Chicken

2 lb. skinless, boneless chicken breasts
3 green onions, thinly sliced
Oil for frying
Chopped cabbage or iceberg lettuce

Mom's Fried Rice

2 eggs
½ lb. bacon, cut into 1-inch pieces
4 cups cold rice
2 tbsp. soy sauce
1 or 2 green onions, thinly sliced

For Marinade: Mix together all the marinade ingredients.

For Paper-Wrapped Chicken: Prepare chicken by pounding out on back side of breasts (between 2 pieces of wax or parchment paper) to break down and tenderize. Cut prepared chicken into small pieces about 2 to 2½ inches long. Mix chicken pieces in the prepared marinade and marinate in the refrigerator for 2 to 3 hours. Mix in green onions.

Cut heavy foil into 24 squares, approximately 5x5 inches. Cut parchment paper into 24 squares slightly smaller than the foil squares. (Precut foil and paper-lined squares may be found at Asian markets.) To wrap the chicken, place foil squares on the counter, and then place a parchment square on each. In the *middle* of each parchment square, place 1 large spoonful of marinated chicken mixture. Fold the bottom right-hand corner of foil up to the top left-hand corner to form a triangle shape with chicken mixture inside. Fold down each side of open triangle with 2 tiny, tight folds. When both sides are folded down, turn both bottom corners up to seal tightly. It is very important to make sure the packets are well sealed so that no oils seeps in and the marinade doesn't seep out!

Heat deep fryer, wok, or your oven to 400 degrees. If using deep fryer (which is preferable), deep fry the packets about 8 at a time, stirring occasionally for about 8 minutes, until the chicken is cooked thoroughly but still moist. Pull out of fryer and drain packets on paper towels. If using wok, fry in oil—in hot wok—for 8 minutes. If using oven, bake on 2 oil-coated baking pans for 10 to 15 minutes, until cooked but still moist.

Serve on a large platter on bed of chopped cabbage or iceberg lettuce. Can be opened and enjoyed with fingers, chopsticks, or a fork and knife. Makes 6 servings.

For Mom's Fried Rice: Lightly beat eggs. Heat a nonstick fry pan and cook the bacon until crisp. Remove bacon from pan and drain on paper towels. Remove half of the bacon fat from the pan. Then add rice to the pan, breaking apart as you stir fry, until heated through. You may also add fresh grated or chopped carrots at this time, if desired. Make a hole in the middle of the warm rice. Cook eggs in the middle of this hole. When eggs are set, mix cooked eggs into rice. Add soy sauce a little at a time to taste. Mix in sliced green onions and crumbled bacon. Serve along with chicken packets. Makes 8 servings.

Tip: To have cold rice, cook rice the day before and refrigerate. You may use brown rice if desired.

Chapter 11

Give Back

Six plump strawberries nestle in a pretty pink box. Two are dipped in milk chocolate, two in dark chocolate, and two in white chocolate. But there are no signature swizzles! Instead, these chocolate strawberries have nipples—yes, nipples. Because these are Breast Berries™. They're made to look like breasts.

We dip a strawberry in one of three colors of chocolate, because women come in different colors, you know? Then we barely dip the tip of the berry into a lighter shade of chocolate to make the areola, and then we place one-half of a sliced Jelly Belly® bean on the tip for the nipple. Each Breast Berry is a one-of-a-kind creation.

Gena, my very best friend since seventh grade, was diagnosed with breast cancer. She underwent a double mastectomy, and although it was a challenging time for her, she is now cancer free. Before Gena's last appointment with her surgeons following the cancer and reconstructive operations, she called me.

"Could you make me two boxes of berries that look like boobs?" she asked. "I want to take them with me to my appointment, to thank my doctors by giving them boobie berries!"

What a great idea! We had previously launched "Breast Cancer Awareness Berries," which were dipped berries wearing an edible pink ribbon and packaged with a cuddly pink beanie bear, also wearing a pink awareness ribbon. We donated a portion of all sales of these berries to breast cancer research. But I'd never thought of making berries actually look like boobs before. It sure sounded fun, though, and also something I could do for Gena to show how much I love her.

Of course, they'd just be special for Gena, I thought. I wouldn't be able to offer them commercially. My berries are strictly G rated!

But then Gena took her boxes of Breast Berries to her doctors and they went nuts over them! "How did you ever get something like that?" they asked in wonder. "Oh, I just made a phone call," Gena said. The nurses loved them too, and when they told other patients about them, those women wanted to know where they could get some. I thought, "Why not make this a tribute to Gena and help raise awareness? They are definitely an attention grabber!"

Women battling cancer don't want to hide and be sad. They want to celebrate when they finish chemo, or when their hair starts to grow back, or when their tests come back normal. A box of Breast Berries says it all—that life is good, and delicious, and to be enjoyed.

In Gena's honor, 10 percent of all Breast Berries purchases will be donated to the Susan G. Komen Foundation for breast cancer research.

* * * *

Although nowadays I give talks to big audiences and go on television and radio shows, I'm not a natural. It used to make me so anxious to speak in front of people—even my little networking group of fifteen women—that I thought I'd throw up. My hands would shake, and the first words barely came out of my mouth.

I still get nervous, although these days I don't have a problem speaking out. No one is making me join the speakers' track, so why am I doing it? Partly because in these days of YouTube and video conferencing, you've got to get used to being in front of people, both in person and on camera. It's the new way to promote yourself, and if you don't promote, you're going to go out of business.

But the main reason why I got on the speakers' track is because I want to give back. I've been so lucky. My favorite thing in the whole world, ever since I was a little kid, was to make people happy. I give thanks every day for the life God has given me.

I give talks because I want to share what has worked for me, in the hope that it might work for others too. It's simply giving back what I have been given. Giving back is one of the most important facets of my life—both my business life and my personal life.

Modeling

When I was a young teenager, one of my dreams was to become

a model (what a glamorous lifestyle, with lots of traveling to exotic destinations!). I had to give up that dream because I wasn't tall and willowy enough. But it came true anyway. I am a different kind of model now—a role model.

Since I started out in the "berry biz," businesses owned by women have multiplied. Twice as many women as men now start new companies. They are helped by the marketing and business-building programs available on the Internet, so they can quickly learn business startup skills and not have to depend completely on the school-of–hard-knocks method. But apart from technology and systems, women also need something else. It was what I needed when I started out and found in people such as Mary Kay Ash and Debbi Fields: other women who started businesses and succeeded beyond their wildest dreams.

Nothing serves to let you know that your dreams are possible more than someone who has accomplished hers. Nothing helps you more than having such a mentor who will tell you *how* she did it. That's what audiences I speak to want to know: how did I create a multimillion-dollar business from scratch, and how can they do it too? They want to know who I am and what I've done, because they need to know if I am just like them.

I've been able to inspire other businesswomen by giving them courage and some hints on how to turn their dreams into reality. Just go for it, I tell them. If I can do it, so can they. My story shows that I *am* like them. When they see me standing at a podium and telling my story, they can see that we are not so different. Maybe they can do it too.

In fact, acting as a role model for other entrepreneurs, both women and men, is my whole reason for writing this book.

Be Yourself

Although I've been told by event organizers and speaking coaches that I am a "natural" at speaking, I know I'm not. But it's true that my message is well received, whether I'm speaking at a business conference, community college, or women's-club meeting. I think they like me because my message is real. I don't try to be anything that I'm not. I'm not polished or perfect. I make some pretty funny mistakes with words. I know who I am—I'm just a berry dipper from Klamath Falls, Oregon.

That doesn't mean I'm not serious about my message. I am. I prepare my remarks beforehand because my anxiety goes down when I do, and I can get my message across more clearly. I learned that you have about fifteen seconds of speaking before the audience decides to tune you out if you're boring or listen if you're interesting. People love stories, so I always tell a story right off the bat, and I usually try to make it a funny one. The story about my dad and the kids with the lemonade stand that I told earlier in this book is one of my favorites.

I prepare 3x5 index cards with one- or two-word reminders of things I know I want to talk about. I found out that the time goes by really fast when you're speaking, and I don't want to be left sputtering, "But wait . . . I haven't told you my Web site yet!" when the MC says, "Thank you, Shari, that was great," and suddenly my time is over.

Sharing Your Knowledge Is Another Win-Win

When I speak to would-be entrepreneurs, one of the things I tell them is to do just what I'm doing right then—speak! Give talks on your specialty, to community organizations, industry conferences, community colleges, churches, networking organizations, business associations, Chamber of Commerce meetings—whatever you can think of. Even if your knees are knocking together, do it anyway. Not only can your expertise and wisdom bring value to someone's life, you will be promoting your business, and yourself as an authority.

And don't be shy of the "big guys." I've appeared on radio and cable TV, and my berries have appeared (with or without me) on the "Today Show," "The Price Is Right," and others. I've spoken to more than a thousand people at a time, at business conferences such as Jennifer Openshaw's Women in the Millionaire Zone in Los Angeles, where I was a speaker alongside Kathy Ireland. (At that one I got a standing ovation, which was pretty darn exciting.) In 2002, I spoke at the California Governor's Conference for Women, also in Los Angeles, and in 2007 and 2010 at the annual event for eWomen-Network in Dallas.

Yet don't forget about talking to the "little guys" either. I speak to business students at Sacramento State two to three times a year. I wake them up by giving them free berry samples, and (no surprise) the feedback I get is always positive. Although once a student was a little disappointed when he asked what my "secret" was for going from a one-woman show to running a big national company. I told him there was no secret; it was just hard work one day at a time. He may have been disappointed in my answer, but he still liked my berries!

It's all about giving back, and at the same time getting your name out there.

Fame

Sometimes when people meet me, they act as if I'm a celebrity or something. I'm no celebrity! I don't deserve any oohs and aahs, although my berries certainly do. In fact, I think one reason why people want to meet me is because I often bring berries with me. This means I get invited to a lot of parties.

Like a lot of teenagers, I had thought I wanted to be rich and famous. Thankfully, we grow up and our dreams expand. Now what I want is for my berries to be famous, my business to be successful, and my family to be comfortable. I don't need expensive vacations or three cars in my driveway. I'm not into status symbols and I live well below my means—to this day I know how to make a dollar stretch.

I try to live the way the Bible says I should, as in Philippians 2:3: "Do nothing out of selfish ambition or vain conceit, but in humility consider others better than yourselves." I don't like stuck-up people, and I sure don't want to be one myself. Besides, when we try to put on a show, that's when God is likely to prune us to make us realize that we're no more special than anyone else. One Saturday afternoon, I had to run to the grocery store, and I went as I was—no makeup, my hair up in a funky bun, wearing faded and stained shorts. When I handed the checker my check, she looked at it and said, in a really loud voice, "Oh wow, you're the berry lady!" Everybody looked up and saw me looking like an absolute slob.

This happened another time too, when my son Hogan was about eleven. On holidays, we always seem to have an abundance of too-small berries that we can't use, and on this Mother's Day I gave them to Hogan, the budding entrepreneur, so he could set up a strawberry stand on a corner of a busy street just a few blocks from our house. I gave him a little walkie-talkie phone so he could call me if he needed something. He hadn't been out there long when he called and said, "Mom, I have to go to the bathroom so bad."

When you gotta go, you gotta go, so I zipped over there. although I was a mess. I'd been planning on a little R&R that weekend, so again I had no make-up, hair all over the place, strawberry juice stains on my shorts—and this time white, unshaven legs to boot. So there I was standing on a corner in the middle of Sacramento, while Hogan rode his bike to our house three blocks away.

A man in a very nice truck drove by, and I saw the driver do a double take when he saw me. He pulled over and stopped, backed up to the strawberry stand, rolled down his window, and asked, "Aren't you Shari herself?" I reluctantly admitted that I was but made him swear never to tell a soul! He laughed and teased that he was going to call in the story to our local newspaper, the *Sacramento Bee*. Great. I looked like a bum selling strawberries on the street corner—while back at my factory, we were shipping out thousands of them. I was embarrassed, but I also have to admit it was pretty funny.

We're all people. We all get dressed in the morning and go to sleep at night. I don't let those oohs, aahs, and standing ovations give me a swelled head. I know I'm still a little hillbilly girl at heart, and one reason why I talk about my roots is because I have never forgotten who I am.

Generosity Runs in the Family

My mom taught my sister, Dayna, and me to be generous and to think of other people before ourselves. But being as unlike as sisters can be, we express it differently. It took us a long time to recognize the strengths in each other's differences.

One of Dayna's favorite stories about me—which she tells all the time—concerns the Easter Bunny. We always got a chocolate bunny in our Easter baskets. Dayna ate hers right away, the very first thing. But I had a hard time eating mine. It was partly because I didn't want to "hurt him," but I also wanted him to last. I ate the chocolate eggs instead and kept my bunny intact. This drove Dayna nuts. She said I'd rather let my bunny turn white and have to throw him away than share him with her. Even worse, she claims this is because I am stingy.

Well, I'm not stingy, although I will admit to being frugal. As kids, Dayna and I went away for a week one summer to Camp Fire

Girls Camp. We are three and a half years apart in age, so she hung out with her friends and I hung out with mine. That year I was finally old enough to climb Mount McLoughlin, which is nearly ten thousand feet high, so I signed up with my friends, as did Dayna and her friends. We had to get up around four o'clock to make it up and down the mountain in one day. All the girls were given the same amount of provisions, which included a canteen of water. Being the cautious and frugal planner that I am, I rationed my water intake, carefully calculating how much I could have on the way up and forecasting what I might need to get me through the trek back down.

Dayna being Dayna, however, she drank all her water before she even got to the top. By the time we got to the summit, she had begun to beg and nag me to share my water with her, which I wouldn't do. I, of course, had enough left. I can hear her now, calling, "Stingy!" after me all the way down that mountain.

Today I sort of wish I had shared my water with her on the mountain, even though it was clearly her fault that she had none left. It would have been more Christian of me to do so. But we were kids and neither of us understood that there are different ways of being generous.

I understand better now. Dayna still thinks I'm stingy in the way I skimp on things she considers important—my boys' haircuts and clothes, for instance. I don't see why I should spend a lot of money on expensive clothes when they only last a couple of months. Boys wear out their clothes pretty fast, and it seems the styles change even faster. As long as the boys are comfortable and happy, that is all that matters to me. But fashion matters to Dayna. She has sons of her own, and she buys them beautiful clothes that last. This means that she hands them down to my boys, which they love and it saves me money. She also cuts my boys' hair, because she is wonderful at it, and the boys love her haircuts too. Everyone wins, except that Dayna still gets ticked off at me because I'd rather save money than have my sons look like male models.

The main difference between us is that Dayna gives even when she has nothing to give. If she only had a dollar, and it was your birthday, she'd spend that dollar on your birthday present. Her theory is that she might die tomorrow, so she might as well spend while she can.

If Dayna invites you to dinner, you can be sure she will have spent more money than she should have and used her time and effort to make that dinner perfect. Her house will look like something out of a magazine, and the food will taste as if it was made by a Top Chef Master. If you're lucky, she'll make her out-of-this-world Banana Cream Pie, which you have to taste to believe. You will find the recipe at the end of this chapter. It's okay with her that I'm sharing it here, and now you too can be blessed by her generosity.

I admire Dayna's generosity, but mine is different. I work hard to make money and invest it wisely, and then I have even more to give. If I die of thirst on the mountain because I drank all my water too soon, how is that going to help anyone else?

Giving Back Is Easy

You can make a big difference with just a little effort. One of my favorite missions came about almost by accident. Clay too has the spiritual gift of giving, and one of the ways he enjoys giving to the community is through people in need, such as the homeless. He goes out of his way to help homeless people who might need a ride, a job for the day or perhaps a meal at McDonald's. There was this one lady he saw all the time pushing her shopping cart along the streets of Sacramento. He'd sometimes give her rides or help her load up her cart. One time he actually bought her a new cart. Another time he asked her what she needed, and she answered, "It would be really nice to have a shower and something to eat." So he just brought her home with him. She was able to take a shower and then had dinner with us. Boy did she eat, but she told us that one of the biggest problems she faced was staying clean.

"What else do you need?" Clay asked. "How about some shampoo and conditioner, or hand cream, or soap?" He said she could have whatever we had in our bathroom.

"Oh no, those bottles are too big and heavy to carry around," she said. "I like the little bottles instead." And I thought, "Oh my gosh, I have a million of those!" Because when you travel for business like I do, those hotel samples of shampoo and conditioner just sort of accumulate in your luggage.

That was the birth of the program that I initiated at all my stores. We collect these little travel-sized bottles of shampoos and soaps, and when we have a bunch, we take them down to the homeless shelters. We display a flyer in our stores, asking people to bring in their samples and travel toiletries to help people in need. Word spread fast. So many people have these things and either stash them in cupboards or just throw them away, and they were delighted to be able to put them to good use. The down-on-their-luck people really love them, and people just feel better when they give to others. I think people are naturally generous.

Miracles don't have to be big. A little bottle of shampoo may be a miracle. We vary our donations; one time they'll go to the Salvation Army, another time to Loaves and Fishes, and so on. I thought we should give some to a women's shelter too, for disadvantaged women trying to get on their feet. One of the women's shelters in downtown Sacramento served a brunch every day, and I often took them leftover berries. I wondered if they might be interested in our mini-toiletries too.

Wellspring Women's Center was established and run by Catherine Connell and Claire Graham, Sisters of Social Service, to provide an environment where personal self-esteem could be nurtured and low-income women might be helped to recognize their innate goodness. I called Sister Catherine just before Easter, when we had hundreds of little bottles that we'd been gathering for some time. When I asked her if she'd be interested in this kind of donation, she excitedly said yes and told me a story.

"We made Easter baskets for the women here," she told me. "The baskets are lovely, but we had nothing to put in them. I didn't want to put in candy because it looked too childish. I wanted something for grown women, something personal that they would really enjoy. Everyone kept asking me, 'Sister, what are we going to put in these baskets?'

"Just today I told them, 'Don't worry. God's going to take care of it.' And then you called. And now those Easter baskets will be filled."

I support my community and the charities that pull at my heart-strings, many of which concern women, children, and animals. I've averaged a donation of over twenty thousand dollars in products every year. I think nearly every fund-raiser or silent auction in Sacramento gives away boxes of my strawberries!

It helps me because I am a part of this community. It helps others because we all need help from time to time. If you open your heart, giving just comes naturally. It's what we are meant to do.

Helping Others Helps You

Although it is not the reason why I give, giving generously has helped build my business brand too. People like to do business with companies of conscience. I want people who buy from the Berry Factory to know that part of the money they spend on gourmet goodies goes to support causes that benefit us all.

My giving list includes at least one hundred charitable organizations: many Sacramento-area schools and churches, Make a Wish, March of Dimes, Crocker Art Museum, Families for Early Autism Treatment (FEAT), Wells, American River College Foundation, Wellspring Women's Center, Little League, Leukemia & Lymphoma Foundation, Easter Seals, American Cancer Society, Shriners' Hospitals, Soroptimist International, WEAVE, PAWS, Junior Diabetes Research Foundation, Prostate Cancer Research Center, and the American Heart Association's Go Red for Women campaign, for example.

I've already written about losing my beloved stepfather, Ben, to prostate cancer, when he was only sixty-one and just about to start on his retirement adventures. After Ben died, I designed a product for Fathers' Day, which we called "Ben's Bouquet," and started donating 10 percent of the sales of this beautiful product to fund prostate cancer research. This program was recently reintroduced on BerryFactory.com.

Ben's Bouquet

The Tuxedo Roses were named "Ben's Bouquet" for one reason. The idea belongs to Ben Starr, Shari's Dad. He thought it was just the right masculine touch to make the long stemmed strawberry roses a suitable gift for men. Ben always wanted his daughter to do more to promote Father's Day. He insisted she was missing a great opportunity to reach a new segment of the marketplace.

The bouquet was introduced on Father's Day 1994, the year after Ben died of prostate cancer, to honor his memory and because it was a darn good idea.

10% of all proceeds from the sale of "Ben's Bouquets" is donated to prostate cancer research.

Someday they will find a cure or prevention for this disease that affects so many men. I did this not only in memory of Ben but also for love of my mom. A few years after Ben died, she married again, and *one month* after they were married her new husband, Ron, was also diagnosed with prostate cancer! I'm so happy to say that he is responding well to treatment, and I like to think that the wonderful work done by doctors such as Eric J. Small at the University of California at San Francisco may have saved Ron's life, so that he and my mom can have many wonderful years together.

I donated my time and a percentage of product sales to the American Heart Association, and in 2009 I got more personally involved, becoming the chairperson for their Go Red for Women movement. We designed a special berry that sports red hearts and swizzles and donated a percentage of its sales to the Go Red cause.

Heart disease is the number-one killer of women in the U.S. More women die of heart disease than the next *fourteen* causes of death combined, including breast cancer. Many of these deaths are preventable, and that's the focus of the Go Red campaign. We want to educate and empower women. This cause has become a passion with me, something I hold close to *my* heart.

Believe it or not, products offered by the Berry Factory are good for your heart and your overall health. Strawberries are full of vitamin C, chocolate in moderation helps with stress, and recently I read that studies show that red wine (also in moderation) might be heart-healthy too!

Another thing that is good for your heart is generosity. Give what you can whenever you can—and you always can.

A Berry Good Tip

Giving as much money as you can afford, to causes you believe in, is good. But giving doesn't always have to cost money. The best giving is when you give of yourself—your time, your energy, your passion, your voice. Giving money is done at a distance, but giving your time gets you known in the community, as a real person. You can share what you know or what you are good at. Teach others how to do what you do. Or volunteer to make phone calls or even sweep the floor. The most important thing is to just show up. You may become a role model for giving. Besides, it's fun.

My favorite community service is to teach people how to dip strawberries into chocolate—what else? The Presbyterian church in my old Sacramento community sponsors a woman's retreat every year, and every year I teach a chocolate-dipping class. Because there can only be twenty people in a class (otherwise it turns into a chocolate disaster), there's always a waiting list—my dipping class is one of the most coveted events. Maybe it has something to do with getting to eat your creations!

I often take my boys with me to do community service. We go to assisted-living facilities and retirement homes and teach chocolate dipping there too, to people in their eighties and nineties. At first the boys were reluctant to go. "It smells in those places," they said, worried.

I told them that even if it does smell, so what? We bring great smells—and tastes, too—with us. My boys have learned to love talking with the old people. They remember Grannie, their great-grandmother, with love, and they've found out how much knowledge, wisdom, and character are waiting for us to learn from those older folks. And all we do is teach them how to dip strawberries in chocolate! We're the ones who should be thanking them.

While we teach how to dip the berries, I usually tell stories about working at the Berry Factory or how I became the "strawberry girl." One time my son Hogan agreed to do part of the talk with me. I said, "Great, you can do it, Hogan!" He was a little nervous, so I made him 3x5 index cards listing the points to cover. He studied them in the car on the way to the retirement home. We got there a little early, and while Hogan set up the chocolate melting vat, the strawberries, and the sprinkles, I put away the extra boxes in the car. When I got back, there were about twenty people sitting in the audience, eagerly listening to Hogan talk. He had started without me!

He really was a natural, not like me. I don't think he even looked at his 3x5 cards. He told the folks about the rules of chocolate dipping—how to hold the berry and how to swirl it around. And then he talked about what he does for the Berry Factory, such as coming up with the name for Caramel Apple Wedgies™, and how he's a chip off the "old block." (The old block is me.) He told them stories about me working my "butt off" on Valentine's Day and what I look like when I come home on the night after Valentine's Day. He had those people eating out of his hand—almost literally!

Giving is even more fun when you get up close and personal.

* * * *

Shari's Secret Recipe #11
Dayna's Banana Cream Pie

9-inch piecrust (see chapter 2)
3 bananas, peeled and thickly sliced
8 oz. cream cheese, room temperature
2 cups milk, divided
1 large pkg. instant vanilla pudding
My Mom's Fresh Whipped Cream (see chapter 6)

Bake and cool the piecrust. Lay bananas into bottom. In a large bowl, blend the cream cheese and ½ cup milk. Add pudding mix and the remaining milk, and beat well. Pour mixture on top of the bananas. Add a layer of fresh whipped cream. Chill at least 1 hour.

Chapter 12

Set the Right Priorities

We just call it the cheese roll. This homespun name does not reflect its glory. Made of orangey velvety cheese that has been flattened into a sheet and slathered with a secret dip made of cream cheese, sour cream, various chopped-up peppers, and have-to-kill-you-if-I-tell-you spices, it is then rolled up, chilled for hours, and served as with crackers and corn chips or stuffed straight into your mouth on the end of a carrot stick. The cheese roll does not last long. Even if your party is small, you have to make more than one.

Have you noticed that most beloved family traditions include food? It's certainly true in my family. When Clay and I got together again, I was introduced to his family's Christmas Eve traditions. Everyone—Clay's parents, his three sisters, and all the spouses and children—gathered at Clay's mom's house on the morning of the twenty-fourth, played through the day, and stayed the night. Donna lived out in the country in a cozy, antique-filled home. We'd spend the morning and afternoon sledding and generally playing outdoors, then pile into a bunch of cars and drive to the home of the Fitzpatricks' friends, the Judds. There we'd have appetizers and cocktails and laugh at anything and everything. After that, we'd pile back into the cars and drive through the dark (and usually the snow) to a little one-room white church with a pointed steeple in Fort Klamath. We'd sit enrapt listening to the traditional Christmas service, which concluded with the congregation singing "Silent Night" by candlelight.

All the traditional activities were wonderful and moving, but I have to admit the one I looked forward to the most was the appetizers at the Judds' home, because of the centerpiece, the cheese roll. It was made by Curt Judd, the son of the Judd family and a childhood buddy of Clay's. Every year I would ask Curt for the trick to making this perfect creation, because I couldn't figure out how to make it myself—it was a mystery to everyone, especially curious me. But Curt said it was a closely guarded family secret that he could not share. He'd smile and say that he didn't want to give it away. He wanted to make sure we'd come back the next year, just so that we could eat the cheese roll again.

But time has a way of moving on, and as the years passed, both Clay's parents and the Judds moved closer in to town. They had to give up the Christmas Eve traditions—and the cheese roll that went with them. One year I ran into Curt Judd and begged him one more time to share the secret of the cheese roll. "I can't look forward to eating it once a year anymore," I wheedled. "I promise I will never tell anyone—it will become my own family party tradition to carry on." I must have sounded pretty desperate, because Curt finally relented!

I am proud that I am one of the only people in the world outside the Judd family who knows how to make the cheese roll. As I promised Curt, it has grown into a new family tradition. If I didn't serve the cheese roll at a family party, I just don't know what would happen—a revolt? Also as I promised Curt, I guard the secrets of the cheese roll closely. You won't find a recipe for it in this book. I'm sorry, but a promise is a promise.

****

The number-one question I'm asked by women entrepreneurs is "how do you run a business and still have a happy family life?" It's a good question. It takes a lot of energy and time to run a business and just as much energy and time to raise children and keep a marriage running smoothly. And you are only human.

I'd love to be home and take care of my family by giving them 100 percent of myself. At the same time, I know I'd miss my business like crazy. I hate that I can't be 100 percent at everything—my business, my marriage, my kids, my home. Sometimes I thought I would go nuts, because when I was at work, I felt as though I should be at home; yet when I was at home, I stressed out because I wasn't taking care of my business. I do the best I can, but it does bother me that I can't commit 100 percent to one thing. I'm not alone; many women suffer from this same guilt.

I'm so glad I am a woman. I think women are great jugglers, which is why we make great businesspeople! We know how to multitask; we've been doing it forever. How we do it is not a secret: choose the correct priorities and put them in the right order.

My pastor once told me that he had never heard anyone on his or her deathbed say that they wish they'd spent more time at the office. Think about that. As much as you love your work, it's still just a *job*. It should not be your *life*. My business supports my family; my family should not suffer because of my work. If God was to take my business from me tomorrow, I would still have the most important things in my life, which are the things you cannot see—love, joy, peace, kindness, goodness, and faithfulness. These are all fruits of the Spirit, as listed in Galatians 5:22.

A great piece of advice I got was from a book written by Mary Kay Ash, of Mary Kay Cosmetics. She said you have to have your priorities straight. Hers were: one, God; two, family; and three, work. When I read that, I knew I had the answer to the problem of guilt. I always put my family before work and God before everything. As it says in Matthew 6:33, "He will give you all you need from day to day if you live for him and make the Kingdom of God your primary concern." That way there's never a decision to make and never any guilt.

Still, it's not easy.

Babies

I was due with my first son, Paxton, around Christmas 1992. Christmas is a busy time for my business, because chocolate-dipped strawberries make great Christmas gifts and elegant contributions to Christmas parties. So I started organizing for the holiday early that year, ordering all my supplies and buying and wrapping all my Christmas presents by October. I was so proud of myself, being a pregnant lady and a businesswoman at the same time.

We didn't go home to Oregon for Christmas that year, because I was too far along to travel. I was big, uncomfortable, and sad because I missed my family and all our Christmas traditions. Even though it was just Clay and me for Christmas Eve dinner, I cooked an eight-pound ham. I looked at it sitting in the middle of the table and thought, "Oh man, that's the size of what's going to come out of me any day now." It seemed impossible.

I felt fine during my pregnancy, but labor was another story. Paxton almost died during labor, in spite of the outstanding care and love of my ob-gyn, Dr. Anne Marie Adams. I will never forget hearing her whisper prayers for Jesus to spare my baby while she was down in front of me delivering him. I had a strep B virus that had gone undetected, and he was born with a severe case of pneumonia. Probably what saved his life was that the top neonatal unit in Sacramento was in the same hospital, so no time was wasted getting him there. He was whisked down the hall, while Clay and I heard shouts of "stat this" and "stat that" that terrified us.

The doctors didn't expect Paxton to live. The hospital chaplain was called to be with us while the doctors explained that even if our baby did live, he would most likely be blind and/or deaf or have major brain damage and certainly cerebral palsy.

That was the day that Clay became a committed Christian, and my faith was strengthened even more. The priorities of life became crystal clear to both of us. Who cared about business, about money, about *anything*? All we needed to be happy was to hold our healthy baby boy in our arms and take him home.

For the next three days, Paxton struggled for his life while we waited for the antibiotics to start working. Due to insurance coverage rules, I was discharged from the hospital and had to go home to a houseful of congratulatory flowers, but no baby. I spent little time there. Nearly all my day was spent sitting by Paxton's crib, only leaving to quickly eat something or take a cat-nap. The nights I spent at home in bed, trying to rest yet waiting for the call from the hospital that would tell me he was gone or slipping away. Thank God that call never came. The neonatal expert, Dr. Callie, monitored Paxton's progress every three hours for those three days. God knows when that doctor slept.

On the third day, it looked as though Paxton would live. He spent the next two weeks in intensive care, but then Clay and I brought home a perfectly healthy baby boy. God is good.

A few years ago, Paxton got to meet Dr. Callie. The hospital held a celebration to honor this great doctor, and all the babies he had saved were invited. Paxton thanked Dr. Callie personally for saving his life, while presenting him with a bouquet of chocolate-dipped strawberries. It was so touching.

Another thing I learned from the drama surrounding Paxton's birth was the importance of being a mature parent even before you are one. Before Clay and I got married, we were both self-employed and didn't want to spend money on health insurance. After all, we were both young and healthy (and dumb). But when we decided to get married, we thought we should be mature now, so in March 1992 I signed us up for insurance. It was to begin on April 1. We were married on April 11 and Paxton was conceived on our wedding night. Nine months later, on January 8, 1993, he was born, and shortly thereafter we received a $100,000 hospital bill. At first, the insurance company wanted to dispute paying the bill, as I had to be covered when the baby was conceived, not when he was born. I explained that only God and I knew when he was conceived, and I was sure that I should be covered. They eventually paid the bill—whew! It was way too close for comfort.

I had easy pregnancies but only one normal labor. That was with my second son, Hogan, who was born eighteen months after Paxton. My third son, Maxwell, also almost didn't survive. During a routine doctor visit three weeks before Max was due, Dr. Adams could not find his heartbeat. She immediately had me rushed to the hospital and induced. The umbilical cord was strangling Max inside of me. The cord had to be cut before he was born, so once he was delivered he also was rushed off to be "jump started." Luckily he didn't have to spend any time in intensive care. That night he was back with me, and we cuddled all night long. The nurses wanted to take him to the nursery so that I could rest, but I wouldn't let them. I wanted him right by my side. My family circle was now complete.

I was lucky that my business was up and running and in its fifth year before Paxton was born. I brought him to work with me often while he was an infant, and I did the same with the other two when they came along. When Paxton was too old to take to work with me, I found a nanny to come to my house three days a week. I've never liked Mondays, so I seldom scheduled any work on Mondays. I spent Tuesdays, Wednesdays, and Thursdays in the office while the nanny was at home with the boys. Nicki, or "Nit" as the boys called her, was sent from God. She cleaned my house, did my laundry, and gave the boys lots of good old TLC when I was away. It was a great balance.

Although I didn't have my babies with me all the time, I still managed to breastfeed all three of them for over a year each. This meant pumping, of course. I usually pumped my breast milk in my office. The pumping noise could be heard all over the store. If a customer asked what the noise was, I grinned and instructed my staff to tell them it was our mixing machine for the milk chocolate!

It's important to keep breast milk fresh, so I carried a little ice chest around with me, even when I was out on deliveries. I was still the main delivery person. I had one full-time employee when Paxton was a baby, so she would man the store while I made deliveries, picked up supplies, and grabbed some lunch. I carried my battery-operated breast pump with me as well as the ice chest. I remember how odd it felt to I pull up to a drive-through window to order my burrito, with my pump going like mad.

A lot of new moms who would like to breastfeed don't, because they think they don't have the time. But I believe there is always a way. My boys' health was my first priority, even if it wasn't convenient at work.

Balance of Power

Here's another question I get asked frequently by aspiring women entrepreneurs: "How does your husband handle your success, and does it impact your marriage?" It's normal to be concerned about the balance of power in a marriage, so this too is a good question.

I was single when I started my business, and I'm grateful for that. I'm not sure I could have lived and breathed my business the way I did those first few years if I'd had a family too.

But maybe I could have. Again, I've been so blessed. Finding the right mate is always a key to happiness, and this is especially true if you're an entrepreneur. I have always been an independent person, and I was a little worried that I might have to give up some of my independence when I married. I remember telling my mom, "I'm so concerned that one day he'll make me furious and I'll be stuck in a marriage with him!" My mom laughed and said, "What, you think there's days when I don't want to just kill Ben? You bet I do! But I don't and I get over it."

Clay always—and I mean always—supports me. He is not jealous of my success. In fact, just the opposite—he's proud of me. Sometimes he's asked how he feels about being "Mr. Berry" and all it does is make him laugh. He calls *himself* Mr. Berry sometimes!

Clay had his own business as a swimming-pool contractor for fifteen years, so he understands the demands of running a business. In the early days of my business, he would often pitch in and help me, especially on Valentine's Day and Mother's Day, our busiest times. He was a big help, but it proved to be not so good for our relationship to work together. He didn't like me bossing him around in front of other people—I am a little stressed out on those days and not quite as sweet as normal. So he doesn't help me out that way anymore, but he does help with new product ideas. Sometimes a great idea will just casually pop out of his mouth, though most of the time I shoot it down. And then six months later he'll be surprised to see it as a new product. He has to remind me and let everyone know that in fact it was his idea.

Clay is a modern husband; he doesn't expect me to be superwoman or to take care of everything to do with the house. I don't have to have dinner on the table at six sharp, and if the house is a mess, the house is a mess. When the boys were small, Clay often bathed them, fed them, and put them to bed, so I could catch up on correspondence or have some time to myself. He changed more than his share of poopy diapers—we sometimes played rock-paper-scissors to see who would have to do the deed and I won more often than not.

We set up a division of labor that works well for us. We don't share a checking account or credit cards; we each have our own monthly financial obligations. Consequently, we've never had a fight about money. Plus we've never shared a bathroom—I think this one is pretty darn important.

We tailor our schedules so that the boys are always taken care of. Clay leaves early in the morning so I get them off to school, and he picks them up and takes care of their needs in the afternoon. He's busy in the summer months when swimming-pool contractors are in demand, but the summer is looser for me, so I take the lead then. His work is slower during the cold wet winter months when I'm slammed with December holidays and Valentine's Day, so he's the lead man then.

And boy, is Clay in charge when it comes to emergencies. I'm just not that good at it; I would make a horrible nurse. I can't stand the sight of blood, and if I have to hurry, I turn into a klutz. If Clay's not around, my first thought is to call my mom, never mind that she lives hundreds of miles away. One time when home alone, I fell down the brick stairs holding the puppy and landed with all my weight on my bare knees. I had blood dripping down my legs and a big toenail had ripped right off, so I called Mom as she was peacefully driving down a country road in Oregon. She told me to call Clay.

Clay takes the lead with raising the boys, too. It's important to us to present a united front to the boys, so they know that we are always together. I knew before we married that Clay was going to be an amazing father. I knew because at family gatherings I could never find him—he was always with the kids, playing football in the street or something. He's like a kid magnet. He has that magical fatherly quality; he's a lot of fun, and at the same time his natural authority makes kids feel safe.

I'm so happy to have three boys who are being raised by a good man to be good men themselves. I used to think I wanted a daughter, too. But now I'm convinced that God knew what He was doing. Having boys is perfect. It gives me my space when they're off doing boy stuff with Clay. I'll wait for granddaughters!

Clay and I constantly tell our boys how proud we are of them, how special they are, and how much we love them no matter what. They are secure and know how lucky they are to have parents who love and enjoy each other.

Clay and I have an equal partnership. I take good care of him and respect him totally. He treasures me and takes good care of me too. My maturing Christian faith has helped this very independent girl accept and understand why being submissive to your husband is God's perfect blueprint for a successful marriage. I can go to him with any problem and share with him every joy. We share the same faith in God, the same dreams, and the same ideas on how to raise our boys. We honor each other's opinions, even when they differ. We never, ever, argue in front of the boys or anyone else. Clay often stresses that it is "you and me against the world." We are a team.

Don't get me wrong. There are times when I do want to kill him, just as I feared before we got married. But we've never had a big fight, only little ones that get resolved pretty quickly. And we've never said anything to each other that we wished later we could take back. Besides, Clay is funny. Right at the point when I begin to think about grabbing a kitchen knife, he'll say something that will make me laugh. And he's really good at saying "sorry" first and has taught me that I need to do that more often. I'm getting better, but I'm still not as good as him.

My business success is founded upon my strong, healthy home life. Even if things go wrong at work, or I have so much stress that my hair is on fire, when I go home I know that I am safe. At home everyone is on my side.

Tradition!

One of the best ways to foster togetherness is to honor the traditions of your family. As you might guess, in my family the traditions nearly always revolve around food. We all have our favorite dishes, and all five of us participate in their preparation. Well, at least all five participate in the eating of them!

The dish I make that my family likes best is chicken saltimbocca. I first tasted this dish at my favorite Italian restaurant, Buca di Beppo. I loved it so much I had to learn to make it myself, and now that I've perfected it I serve it at many special family dinners. It takes a lot of preparation but is well worth it. I've convinced my boys (all four of them, counting Clay) to help me with different steps over the years. I'll have one boy pounding the chicken flat (this seems to be their favorite task; I guess it appeals to their masculine nature), another boy finely chopping the fresh sage and lining the chicken with prosciutto, another boy squeezing lemons for the fresh lemon juice needed for the sauce, and the final boy giving orders to the other three. I hope that all the boys will learn every step and share it with their own families in the years to come.

I'm not the only one who cooks in our family. Clay has gotten into the act, and he is surprisingly good, especially when we go camping. I already turned you on to his fabulous camping desserts. The boys always get a fire going early to make sure Dad has great coals to cook with. One of Clay's best ideas was "hobo dinner." This is a hodgepodge of anything and everything, including raw meats such as steak chunks, chicken pieces, or sliced hot dogs; vegetables such as baby carrots, tater tots, onions, or canned beans; and a dab of butter and any spices you want to throw in the mix. Then you put all of your chosen ingredients in a tin container, mark it with your indentifying initials, wrap it up with foil, and toss it in the coals to cook until done. Clay supervises the tins in the fire, but he always says, "If you don't like it, it's your own fault," because everyone gets to choose what to put in their own tin. We've had some pretty strange concoctions over the years, but somehow they all get eaten no matter what they look like.

Give Clay foil and some coals, and he is just unbeatable. I married a genius.

Juggling

Even with a supportive husband and a nanny when the boys were small, I've had to do a lot of juggling, like all working mothers. It comes with the territory.

I'm so grateful to be living now, when technology makes it possible for me to do much of my work from home. I get bored easily, so I love it that my schedule changes a lot. Most days I'm here to feed the boys their breakfast and get them off to school with a sack lunch, and I am often here when they get home so I can hear about their day.

My boys' comfort and happiness is one of my main priorities. I've learned that the way to a boy's heart is simple—just feed him! It doesn't have to be fancy; it just has to be food and lots of it. Those stories about teenage boys' appetites are totally true.

I do have to travel from time to time and cannot take my sons with me. (Although when we travel on vacation, I *always* take them with me—it wouldn't be a vacation without my boys!) When I'm on a business trip, I try to be gone as few school days as possible. I work hard to make sure everything is organized while I'm gone: rides, carpools, school projects, sports practices, and so on. I leave detailed daily notes for each of them with reminders about taking their vitamins, what time to leave for school, and stuff like that. They do great while I'm away and always have, even when they were little. They've been raised to be independent. (Clay says that I do too much for them and they actually are more independent when I'm away.)

These days they get themselves up, make their breakfast, take care of the dogs, make their lunches, lock up the house, and get to the bus all on their own. I usually call and talk to each of them every morning I'm gone. It's not to check up on them, because I know they are fine, but just to hear their voices say, "Love you, Mom." And of course they always know how to reach me.

I've always liked to travel, so if I'm gone for four to five days for my business, I enjoy myself, secure in the knowledge that everything at home is just fine. Yet I am careful not to travel too much. I've learned how to say no to unnecessary evening business functions and trips. I always ask myself if it is absolutely necessary for my business that I attend an event or take a trip. If it isn't, I just don't go.

Or I look for that win-win I know is there somewhere. I once was scheduled to speak at a conference in Anaheim, California, and was approached by the Anaheim Chamber of Commerce to speak at their breakfast meeting the day after the conference ended. I thought, "That will put me away from home for six days—that's just too long." So I passed. But then the chamber called me and said, "How about if we bring your whole family with you and put you up at Disneyland?" That worked out great—we all stayed through the weekend, I didn't have to be away from my family, and I got to speak at another event.

If you look at it the right way, juggling can be fun.

A Family Business

The best way to have a successful business and a successful family life is to integrate them together. Letting your kids help you with your work is a great way to teach them good values—honesty, tenacity, creativity, hard work. My business is truly a family business.

For one thing, boys make excellent tasters and critics! If I'm developing a new product, the first thing I do is bring it home. If it doesn't pass my boys, I don't put any more energy into it. If they don't like it, I'm pretty sure no one else will either.

I need honest tasters. I need people to tell me the truth and not worry about hurting my feelings. I can trust my boys to deliver that honesty. They know that I won't sulk or get defensive and that I really want to know what they think. They know that I take their opinions seriously.

The boys have also helped me on special piecework projects that I bring home from time to time, such as stuffing envelopes, cutting ribbons, or folding boxes. They know the layout of my gift cupboard nearly as well as I do. And of course they are all expert chocolate dippers by now because of all the prototypes we've experimented with.

They have grown up with my business, so it's a part of who they are. They take "our" business to school with them. Starting with Paxton in kindergarten, and continuing every year for each boy since then, on the first day of school the boys take a box of berries with them for the teacher, and they enjoy the teacher's reaction when she finds out who they are. At the end of each school year, I come into their classrooms and bring all the goodies needed for the whole class to dip strawberries, cookies, and licorice and to make fancy little boxes to put them in. I tell my story and give away prizes. They boys—and all their friends—just love it.

It only took a couple of years for the teachers to start jockeying to get one of the Fitzpatrick boys in their class, because they know they'll get berries all year round—the beginning-of-the-year gift, the Christmas gift, the teacher-appreciation gift . . . and of course the end-of-the-year dipping party. My boys are pretty popular with their teachers.

They're popular with their friends, too. They are proud of our family business and proud of me too. They've grown used to having a "famous" mom, and now they count on it. Actually, I think they flaunt it.

When Paxton was in eighth grade, though, he suddenly decided that the dipping party at the end of the year wasn't cool anymore. It was embarrassing, he said, and asked me not to come. So I didn't. I did Hogan's and Max's classes that year, because they were still in grade school and not so bothered about being cool.

I didn't find this out until the following year, but Paxton's friends were not happy that I didn't come to their class that year. "Where's your mom?" they asked him. "Hey, what's up with your mom not doing the berry party?" They were disappointed and let Paxton know it.

The next year, as a ninth-grade freshman in high school, Paxton came to me and said, "Mom, because you didn't do eighth grade, I want you to come twice this year. You owe me one." Hmmm, all of a sudden I was cool again.

Now Paxton is the "berry guy" at school. He's on the golf team and he's got a golf shirt with the Berry Factory logo on it. My company sponsored his baseball team one year. And of course if it's somebody's birthday, his friends expect Paxton to show up with berries.

Paxton recently called me at work. "Mom, can you bring home a box of berries?" he asked. "My buddy has been driving me to golf all week, so I promised him some berries."

"Okay," I said, and we hung up.

He called back. "Actually, it's his brother's birthday, too. He wanted to know if he could have some berries."

"Okay, no problem, I'll bring two boxes."

"And there's this girl. I need a box for her because it's her birthday too. So bring three."

"What kind of girl?" I asked. I was curious, I admit it. Paxton hadn't brought home a girlfriend yet. What can I say—I'm a mother.

"No, Mom," he replied. "She's just a friend."

I used to tease my boys that when they got older and started dating, I'd wonder if the girl really loved them or if she was just in it for the berries. Now my teasing was coming true!

Family Inspiration

My berry products have always been inspired by my family. I think of products that I want to give to people I love, and I figure that my customers will want to give those products to those they love. One of my most popular gifts are Tuxedo Berries, berries dipped and decorated to look like the front of tuxedos, featured on Father's Day to honor my beloved stepfather, Ben. And on Mother's Day I always try to think of new products to feature, because my mom is so special to me. So is my mother-in-law, who sends *me* gifts on Mother's Day to thank me for taking care of her son!

My marketing is inspired by my family also. I take my sons with me to events often. Many times I've included them in my business. Photos of the boys and me have appeared in print ads and on our Web site. Hogan has done the voice for our Mother's Day radio ads. He's also worked the Berry Factory booth at the California State Fair. He's so personable and enthusiastic that he draws a crowd every time.

Paxton too is excellent with words. Because I'm always being asked to mentor entrepreneurs, I decided to start a small consulting business. I needed a name for this little side business. I explained my idea at home, and Paxton immediately asked, "How about Shari's Secrets?" It was a great name, and it just rolled off his lips. I've started to show him all my PR stuff now, and he's really good. He'll say, "Mom, it's just too complicated. Keep it simple."

Even Max, young as he is, has sharp opinions about advertising. Recently he examined an ad we had in the paper and remarked, "You know, Mom, that ad really should have been in color." And he was right.

I bring home ads, press releases, ideas for naming a new line, you name it, and I run them by my boys for their opinions. This is good for them—it builds their confidence and encourages their creativity. And it's also good for business, because kids are a lot smarter than adults give them credit for. Their ideas are almost always good ones.

There is no question that my family is more important than my business. But sometimes, when I'm lucky, they merge together and make each other stronger.

A Berry Good Tip

God has a plan for me. I walk in faith that I am doing His will. I can make mistakes, but I cannot stray far off the path if I keep my priorities straight: God, family, work, in that order. My business decisions are no longer hastily made. The same goes for decisions I make regarding my family. I only make decisions after lots of prayer, and I recommend this to anyone. I dedicated my business and my family to God years ago. I feel that the Berry Factory is God's company. I know that God will take care of me and the people I love.

God is the best business partner anyone can have, especially right around Valentine's Day! February 12, 13, and 14 are big prayer days for me, I can tell you. I'm extra busy on those days, so my prayers are pretty simple. I just pray that I will feel His arms around me all day long.

My business success and my wonderful family life seem magical to me, as though sprinkled with pixie dust. But I know there's nothing magic about it. It's God, pure and simple. He saw that my special talent was making people feel good, so I was led to this path. Rick Warren, in his book *The Purpose Driven Life,* said, "Life is a temporary assignment." Clay, my three sons, and my business—these make up my assignment here on earth.

God doesn't promise us an easy life. He gives us the tools to live a good life, but it's up to us to figure out how to use those tools. I've been able to keep my optimistic attitude through difficult times because I know that God has a plan for me. All He wants is for me to do the best I can as I try to follow that plan.

I pray for guidance every single day. All of us need guidance. Because no one does anything alone.

* * * *

Shari's Secret Recipe #12
Shari's Chicken Saltimbocca

4 (6 oz. each) boneless, skinless chicken breasts

Salt to taste
Pepper to taste
2 tbsp. minced fresh sage
4 thin slices prosciutto
2 tbsp. olive oil
Flour for dusting
¼ cup chicken stock
¼ cup white wine
2 tbsp. fresh lemon juice
½ can quartered artichoke hearts, drained (canned in plain water, not oil or marinated)
2 oz. drained capers
1 tbsp. cream or half-and-half
4 tbsp. unsalted butter, room temperature
4 lemon wedges

Flatten chicken breasts to ⅛-inch thickness by pounding lightly between 2 sheets of wax paper. Sprinkle each piece with salt and pepper and spread top of each evenly with sage.

Top each breast with 1 slice prosciutto. (Most recipes for this dish say to secure the prosciutto to the chicken with wooden toothpicks, but it is a hassle to pull these toothpicks out of the cooked, hot chicken. I've found that the prosciutto will automatically stick to the chicken breasts when you first cook them with the prosciutto side down, as follows.)

Heat the oil in a large skillet over medium heat. Dust each breast with flour and place in the skillet prosciutto side down. Cook until golden brown. Turn chicken over and finish cooking, about 8 minutes. Place the chicken on a baking sheet and cover with foil to keep warm.

Discard oil from skillet and add chicken stock, wine, lemon juice, artichokes, capers, and salt and pepper to taste. Cook for 8 to 18 minutes and remove from heat. Mix in the cream and butter to thicken sauce. If it is too thin, add a small amount of flour to thicken. Put back on heat just to warm the sauce.

Place chicken on a large platter, prosciutto side up, and pour sauce over it. Garnish platter with lemon wedges. Serve immediately. *Fantastico!*